GW00771513

Enjoy the walks, and may the sun shine all day, your boots feel comfortable on your feet and your pack feels as light as a feather! Happy walking! John N. Merrill

Something to ponder.

As we walk around this amazing world, we take for granted the stunning diversity of life and nature. We pass the slopes of mountains and the river valleys. We see birds, insects, animals and all the kaleidoscope of flowers and trees. But let's stop for a moment and just stand in awe of this plethora of sights. However hard we, as humans try, we cannot match the magnificence that our eyes see. Whether you are spiritual or not, you cannot ignore or be moved to wonder at the incredible work of a higher dimension - the divine.

While many would say this is evolution, there still has be "someone", who first thought up the flower, tree, bird, animal, and landscape. You only have to gaze at a small mountain flower and see the delicate stems and petals made to perfection. Whilst the earth's movement have created our landscape, the forces of the divine have been at work to help create that breathtaking view. We on the other-hand have been given eyes and feelings, so that we can appreciate and stand in awe at the sight before us.

So as we wander down a path in woodland or high mountains, where the whole spectrum of life is laid out for us to see. Lets give eternal thanks for being able to walk and see these things first hand. To be able to touch, feel and appreciate the work of the divine, makes the effort more than worthwhile. So, as you walk, stop and ponder at the never ending variety of sights and smells that confront us on each stride we take.

John N. Merrill 2014

The Art of walking the John Merrill Way.

1. Always set off in the clothes you plan to wear all day, given the weather conditions. Only on sudden changes in the weather will I stop and put on a waterproof or warmer clothing.

2. Set off at a steady comfortable pace, which you can maintain all day. You should end the walk as fresh as when you started.

3. Maintain your pace and don't stop. Stopping for any period of time disrupts your rythmn and takes upwards of a mile (20 mins) to settle back down into the flow/ease of movement.

4. Switch your phone off. Listen and enjoy the countryside - the smell of the flowers, bird song, the rustle of leaves and the tinkling stream, and observe the wildlife.

5. Ignore the mileage and ascents - don't tick the miles or hills, just concentrate on what the walk's goal is. To think otherwise slows you down and makes the walk a struggle rather than a joy. In a similar vein, when ascending just keep a steady pace and keep going. To stop is to disrupt the flow and make the ascent interminable.

6. Whist a walk is a challenge to complete, it is not just exercise. You should enjoy the world around you, the flowers, birds, wildlife and nature and look at and explore the historical buildings and churches that you pass. Industrial complex's have their own beauty. All are part of life's rich tapestry.

7. Remember that for every mile you walk, you extend your life by 21 minutes.

8. A journey of a 1,000 miles begins with a single step and a mile requires 2,000 strides.

"The expert traveller leaves no footprints" Lao Tzu.

THE JOHN MERRILL FOUNDATION LONG DISTANCE WALKING CHARTER FOR THE UK.

1. All path signs to be made of wood and clearly state the right of way designation and destination, with correct mileage/kilometers. Individually designed, logo or symbols is to be encouraged. Variety and individuality is essential.

2. Wooden stiles are preferred to kissing gates. Kissing gates have a fatal flaw - many are not wide enough yo allow a backpacker with his pack to get in and out of without removing the pack. For half the year the central area is wet and muddy. The metal bar stiles with a wide base and narrow neck at thew top should be abolished; they are not suitable for backpackers - all have to take the rucksacks off to get through.
SOS - *Save our stiles* - part of our heritage.

3. All long distance routes to clearly state the start and end of the route on the ground, with an overall map showing the route at each end. Registration boxes at either end for signing in and out.

4. All long distance routes should provide regular places for wild camping. No ammenities required just a place to pitch a tent.

5. All temporary path closures should be notified from the nearest road and not at the start of a particular path - this results in having to walk back. The diversion or temporay alternative route should be clearly well signed.

6. Every walker should be trained to read a map, use a compass and calculate a gride reference. The dependence of modern technology is to be encouraged - but learn the basic skills.

7. All long distance walkers should wear well broken in and good fitting boots, wkith two pairs of socks, and carry the minumum basics in a suitable padded and framed rucksack.

8. All footpaths & rights of way's should be be regularly cleared of brambles, nettles, blow downs, and overhanging branches to allow a walker to pass through comfortably. Paths should be natural earth, not gravel, tarmac or rock slab.

9. Take your rubbish home - pack it in, pack it out.

10. Take only pictures.

11. Admire the flowers but do not pick them.

12. Say "hello" to all walkers that you pass.

13. Leave your headphones, music centre at home so you can enjoy the sounds of nature. Switch your phone off and only use in an emergency.

HELP ME TO KEEP THE
WALK GUIDES UPTO DATE.

This guidebook instructions were correct when written and I have detailed what I have found on my walk. But the countryside changes – stiles become kissing gates; inns change their names or are closed down. Paths are diverted, new roads are made, and path signs are often vandalised.

I endeavour to keep upto date with the changes but with about 450 guidebooks covering some 8,600 routes it is a never ending task. I do completely rewalk the routes and write totally new books about a specific walk or route, but it takes time. If you do one of the walks in this book and you find an error or an amendment, would you inform me? The update will be added to book immediately and you will receive a signed copy of the updated book, as a thank you gift.

Your help is greatly appreciated.

Happy walking!
John
Email – marathonhiker@aol.com

The John Merrill Foundation

- is a not for profit charitable Foundation, solely committed to ensuring the copyright, moral rights and writings of Revd. John Merrill are available to all.

The book was originally published by John Merrill and went through numerous reprintings. This Print-on-Demand edition was first printed in 2017.

All rights reserved.

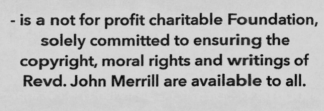

Walking the Canals of LONDON

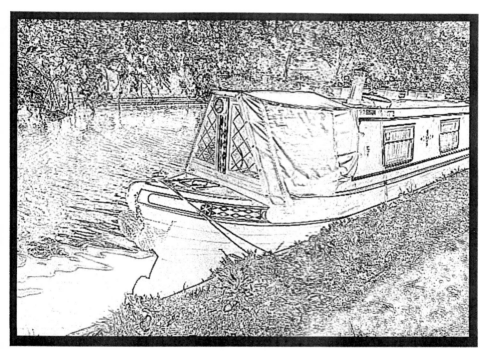

by Revd. John N. Merrill

THE CANAL WALKS SERIES - Vol. 16.

"Hiking the sacred paths & trails of the world for others to enjoy".

THE JOHN MERRILL FOUNDATION

THE JOHN MERRILL FOUNDATION
32, Holmesdale, Waltham Cross,
Hertfordshire, England. EN8 8QY

Tel/Fax - 01992-762776
E-mail - john@johnmerrillwalkguides.co.uk
www.johnmerrillwalkguides.co.uk
www.thejohnmerrillministry.co.uk
www.londoninterfaithchurch.co.uk

International Copyright © John Merrill . All rights reserved. No part of this publication may be reproduced or transmitted in any form or by any means electronic or mechanical including photocopy, recording or any information storage or retrieval system in any place, in any country without the prior written permission of The John Merrill Foundation.

John N. Merrill asserts their moral rights to be identified as the authors of this work.

A catalogue record for this book is available from the British Library.

Conceived, edited, typset and designed by *The John Merrill Foundation*
Printed and handmade by *John N. Merrill.*
Book layout and cover design by *John N. Merrill*

© Text and photographs - by Revd. John N. Merrill 2013
© Maps by Revd. John N. Merrill, HonMUniv, R.I.M.A. 2013
© Additional material - Revd. John N. Merrill, HonMUniv, 2013.

ISBN 978 - 0-9553691-2-4
First Published - June 2006. Revised and reprinted - May 2013.
Special limited edition.

Typeset in Humanst521 - bold, italic, and plain 11pt, 14pt and 18pt
Main titles in 18pt .**Humanst521 Bd BT** by John Merrill in Adobe Pagemaker on a iMac.

Please note - *The maps in this guide are purely illustrative. You are encouraged to use the appropriate 1:25,000 O.S. Explorer map as detailed on each walk.*

John Merrill confirms he has walked all the routes in this book and detailed what he found. Meticulous research has been undertaken to ensure that this publication is highly accurate at the time of going to press. The publishers, however, cannot be held responsible for alterations, errors, omissions, or for changes in details given. They would welcome information to help keep the book up to date.

Cover design & photo's © The John Merrill Foundation 2013.
Photographs by Revd. John N. Merrill.

The John Merrill Foundation maintains the John Merrill Library and archives and administers the worldwide pubishing rights of John Merrill's works in all media formats.

Printed on paper from a 100% sustainable forest.
The John Merrill Foundation plants sufficient trees through the Woodland Trust to replenish the trees used in its publications.

John high up the Lake District - June 2017.

A little about Revd. John N. Merrill

John is unique, possessing the skills of a marathon runner, mountain climber and athlete. Since his first 1,000 mile walk through the islands of the Inner and Outer Hebrides in 1970, he has since walked over 219,000 miles and worn out 133 pairs of boots, 49 rucksacks and more than 1,600 pairs of socks. He has brought marathon walking to Olympic standard. In 1978 he became the first person to walk around the entire coastline of Britain - 7,000 miles. He has walked across Europe, the Alps and Pyrenees - 3,000 miles with 600,000 feet of ascent and descent. In America he has walked the 2,500 mile Appalachian Trail; the Pacific Crest Trail - 2,500 miles in record time; the Continental Divide Trail; became the first person to thru-hike the Buckeye Trail - 1,350 miles in Ohio and completed a unique 4,260 mile walk in 178 days coast to coast across America. He has climbed all the mountains in New Mexico and walked all the trails.

In Britain he has walked all the National Trails many times; linked all the National Parks and trails in a 2,060 mile walk; completed a 1,608 mile Land's End to John o' Groats walk and countless other unique walks. He has walked three times to Santiago de Compostella via different routes; to St. Olav's Shrine in Norway - 420 miles; walked to Assisi, St. Gilles du Gard, the Cathar Ways and to Mont St. Michel. He has walked every long distance path in France and Germany, and walked to every pilgrimage destination in England and France, and extensively walked in every country in Europe.

He has walked in Africa; all the trails in the Hong Kong Islands; and completed five trekking expeditions to the Himalyas and India. Not only is he the world's leading marathon walker he is Britain's most experienced walker. John is author of more than 440 walk guides which have sold more than 4 million copies with more than 1 million sold on the Peak District. He has created more than 80 challenge walks which have been used to raise, so far, more than a £1 million for different charities.

John has never broken a bone or been lost and never had any trouble anywhere. He still walks in the same body he was born with, has had no replacements and does not use poles. This he puts down to his deep spiritual nature and in 2010 he was ordained as a multi-faith Minister - a universal monk, "honouring and embracing all faiths and none". He conducts weddings and funerals services all over UK and abroad. He teaches Qigong and is a Reiki practioner. He gives illustrated talks on his walks all over the U.K.

CONTENTS

Page No.

Introduction 7
About City Walking 8
City Walking Equipment Notes 9
Enjoy the Waterways in Safety 10
Canal Features - what to look for 11
Regent's Canal -
Brief History notes 12
Regent's Canal - Limehouse basin to Islington Tunnel - 4 miles 14
Mini Canal Ring - Regent's, Hertford Union & River Lee
Navigation - 6 miles 20
Islington to Little Venice - 4 1/2 miles 24
Little Venice to Islington, via River Thames - 8 miles 36
Grand Union Canal -
Brief History Notes 42
The Grand Union Canal - Paddington Branch - Little Venice
to Alperton - 6 1/2 miles 44
Alperton, Grand Union Canal and Brent River - 17 miles 48
Grand Union Canal, Hanwell Flight, Osterley Park,
Syon House and River Thames - 12 miles....................58
The River Thames Notes & the London Loop - 24 miles................69
River Thames - Richmond to Westminster - 18 miles 70
River Thames - Westminster to Limehouse Basin - 6 miles 82
Isle of Dogs, River Thames, Woolwich, Greenway and
the Limehouse Cut - 20 miles.........................86
U.K. Canal Museums 98
Walk Record Chart 99
Canal Walk Badge Order Form 100
Other Canal Books by John N. Merrill 101
Other books by John N. Merrill 103

The Limehouse Basin - Lock to the River Thames and where the Regent's Canal and River Lee Navigation start from.

INTRODUCTION

I first began walking the "London" canals beside my home, on the River Lee Navigation, and was surprised at the peaceful nature of them so close to the capitol. As time progressed I walked south to Limehouse Basin and the River Thames and discovered more absorbing historical walking.

So, with the River Lee and River Stort Navigation's fully walked and written about, it was time to head west and explore the Regent's Canal and the Paddington Branch of the Grand Union Canal. Again fascinating walking through Camden Town and Regent's Park to Little Venice. Then on along the Grand Union to its junction with the main Birmingham bound canal. Surprisingly, I saw few walkers but plenty of wildlife - fox's, squirrels, grey herons, canada geese, mallard ducks, coots and moorhens, but only one kingfisher. From the junction at Bull's Bridge I headed to the River Thames and the Hanwell flight of locks. The walking is flat and some walks are long, but being in London you are never far from public transport - bus or train - so you can "quit" when you want and come back another day and complete the walk.

Some walks are circular - around Hanwell Locks via Syon Park and through the delightful River Brent Valley Park. To complete the water theme, I have walked the River Thames from Richmond to Limehouse Basin, to make a water circuit of some 50 miles; which you can do in stages.

One final walk explores the Isle of Dogs, Greenwich and the Thames Barrier, before returning to the Limehouse basin via the River Lee Navigation; thus coming full circle.

Another canal book is complete but the London canal story isn't, for now I continue on along the Grand Union Canal, following it through the Colne Valley....my work and walking never ends!

Enjoy these walks in this fine capitol city and see it from a different perspective.

Happy walking!

John Merrill

ABOUT CITY WALKING
- some personal thoughts.

Whilst every care is taken detailing and describing the walks in this book, it should be borne in mind that the countryside changes by the seasons and the work of man. I have described the walk to the best of my ability, detailing what I have found on the walk in the way of stiles and signs. Obviously with the passage of time stiles become broken or replaced by a ladder stile or even a small gate. Signs too have a habit of being broken, pushed over or obliterated by graffiti. All the route follow rights of way and only on rare occasions will you have to overcome obstacles in its path, such as a temporary closed path because of repair work. On rare occasions rights of way are re-routed and these amendments are included in the next edition. Inns have a frustrating time of changing their name, then back to the original one!

The seasons bring occasional problems whilst out walking which should also be borne in mind. In the height of summer countryside paths can become overgrown and you may have to fight your way through in a few places. In summer the ground is generally dry but in autumn and winter, especially because of our climate, the surface can be decidedly wet and slippery; sometimes even gluttonous mud!

These comments are part of countryside walking which help to make your walk more interesting or briefly frustrating. Standing up to your ankles in mud might not be funny at the time but upon reflection was one of the highlights of the walk!

The mileage for each section is based on three calculations -

1. pedometer reading.
2. the route map measured on the map.
3. the time I took for the walk.

I believe the figure stated for each section to be very accurate but we all walk differently and not always in a straight line! The time allowed for each walk is on the generous side and does not include any sight seeing, refreshment stops or pub stops. The figure is based on the fact that on average a person walks 3 miles an hours but less in hilly terrain. Allow 20 minutes to walk a mile; ten minutes for 1/2 mile and five minutes for 1/4 mile.

Walking in the London area is naturally flat and a good public transport system operates. On most walks you are never far from a bus stop or underground/ train station. If you feel you have had enough and only done part of the walk; stop and go home and come back another day. There is no shame in only doing part of the walk; it is better to have walked part of it than not at all.

CITY WALKING EQUIPMENT NOTES - some personal thoughts.

Today there is a bewildering variety of walking gear, much is superfluous to general walking in Britain. As a basic observation, people over dress for the outdoors. Basically equipment should be serviceable and do the task. I don't approve of walking poles; humans were built to walk with two legs! The following are some of my throughts gathered from my unique walking experiences.

FOOTWEAR -   For summer use I wear walking trainers and in winter lightweight boots. I prefer a good quality boot with a full leather upper, of medium weight, with a vibram sole. I always add a foam cushioned insole to help cushion the base of my feet.

SOCKS - I generally wear two thick pairs as this helps minimise blisters. The inner pair are of loop stitch variety and approximately 80% wool. The outer are a thick rib pair of approximately 80% wool.

CLOTHES & WATERPROOFS - for general walking I wear a T shirt or cotton shirt with a cotton wind jacket on top, and shorts - even in snow! You generate heat as you walk and I prefer to layer my clothes to avoid getting too hot. Depending on the season will dictate how many layers you wear. In soft rain I just use my wind jacket for I know it quickly dries out. In heavy or consistant rain I slip on a poncho, which covers my pack and allows air to circulate, while keeping dry. Only in extreme conditions will I don overtrousers, much preferring to get wet and feel comfortable. I never wear gaiters!

FOOD - as I walk I carry bars of chocolate, for they provide instant energy and are light to carry. In winter a flask of hot coffee is welcome. I never carry water and find no hardship from not doing so, but this is a personal matter! From experience I find the more I drink the more I want and sweat. You should always carry some extra food such as trail mix & candy bars etc., for emergencies.

RUCKSACKS - for day walking I use a climbing rucksack of about 40 litre capacity and although it leaves excess space it does mean that the sac has a well padded back, padded shoulder straps, and a raincover. Inside apart from the basics for one day, including a camera, in winter I carry gloves, spare pullover and a pair of socks.

MAP - when I am walking I always have the relevant map - preferably 1:25,000 scale - open in my hand. This enables me to constantly check that I am walking the right way.

9

British Waterways

Enjoy the Waterways in Safety

Please Do

- make sure your boat has a valid licence
- navigate with care and consideration and observe the speed limit
- make sure your bicycle has a valid permit
- follow the instructions of British Waterways employees

Please Do Not

- swim or paddle
- fire guns or throw stones
- leave litter or pollute the waterway
- obstruct the towpath
- ride a horse (unless on a designated bridle way) or a motorcycle
- interfere with locks sluices or bridges

This is a summary of British Waterways Bye-laws which can be inspected at any Waterway office. Non-observance may result in prosecution.

CANAL FEATURES TO LOOK FOR -

STOP PLANKS - In various places can be seen vertical grooves in the canal walls - especially near bridges - with handled planks stacked nearby. The planks are slotted into the grooves sealing the canal while repairs or cleaning of a drained section is carried out.

ROPE GROOVES - on the side of the bridges, sometimes with either cast iron or wooden shields, can be seen the grooves cut by the horse tow lines over the decades. A memory of how boats were carried along the canal. Several bridges on the Regent's Canal, especially near Camden Town, show rope grooves.

TURNOVER/CROSSOVER BRIDGES - In a few places the towpath switches sides of the canal and a bridge was built to enable the horse to cross over without unhitching the line. The River Lee Navigation has a splendid examples.

SWING BRIDGES - As the name implies, the bridge could be swung out across the canal or swung to the side to allow boats to pass.

BALANCED BRIDGES - Bridges finely balanced that can be either pushed upwards out of the way or lowered across the canal for people, tractors and cattle to cross.

SKEW BRIDGES - Most canal bridges are built at right angles to the canal. In a few cases to avoid the Z bend in the road, the bridge was built at an angle.

MILEPOSTS - Not every canal has mileposts, but there are path signs giving the mileage.

LOCK AND BRIDGE NUMBERS - Not every Canal/Navigation numbers them; many just rely on their name. The Regent's Canal has small plaques on the bridges. On the River Lee Navigation the locks are numbered as is The Grand Union Canal - from Birmingham to the River Thames.

POUND - The length of canal between two locks.

WINDING HOLE - A small area/arm of the main canal, usually near a lock, for turning the narrowboat round.

REGENT'S CANAL
- BRIEF HISTORY NOTES -

8 1/2 miles long. 9 locks and two tunnels - Islington Tunnel - 960 yards and Maida Hill Tunnel 272 yards.

Runs from Limehouse Basin to Little Venice Basin, near Paddington on the Paddinton Branch of the Grand Union Canal, and was opened on August 1st. 1820. Descends 86 ft. / 26 meters from Little Venice to Limehouse basin. The final building cost was double the original budget at £772,000. 1956 was the year when horse drawn commercial traffic was last used the canal.

The canal was first proposed in 1802 by Thomas Homer. It wasn't until 1811 that he approached John Nash about the idea. He was building Regent's Park and agreed to design.the canal and although originally planned to go through the park, he thankfully changed his mind and made go around it. He was a good friend of the Prince Regent after whom the canal and park were named. Work began in October 1812 with James Morgan as the engineer. The section from Paddington to Camden was opened in 1816.

Islington Tunnel and Maida Hill tunnels have no towpath and horses were led over the top. Today the pavement has blue plaques to follow as you walk from end of the tunnel to the other. All canals are different and the Regent's Canal is no exception with plaques on every bridge giving the road name. The locks are not numbered but simply named.

Regent's Canal - Maiden Lane Bridge plaque.

Islington Tunnel over head path sign in the pavement.

REGENT'S CANAL - LIMEHOUSE BASIN TO ISLINGTON TUNNEL - 4 MILES

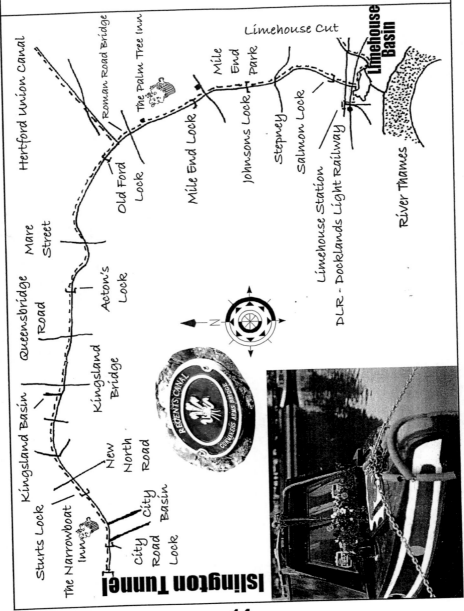

Limehouse Basin

Limehouse Cut

Hertford Union Canal

Roman Road Bridge

The Palm Tree Inn

Mile End Park

Old Ford Lock

Mile End Lock

Johnsons Lock

Stepney

Salmon Lock

Limehouse Station

DLR - Docklands Light Railway

River Thames

Mare Street

Queensbridge Road

Acton's Lock

Kingsland Basin

Kingsland Bridge

New North Road

Sturts Lock

The Narrowboat Inns

City Road Basin

City Road Lock

Islington Tunnel

N

REGENTS CANAL

CUNNINGS ARMS BRIDGE

REGENT'S CANAL - LIMEHOUSE BASIN TO ISLINGTON TUNNEL
- 4 miles
- allow 2 hours. One way walk.

Basic route - Limehouse Basin - Regent's Canal - Mile End Park - Roman Road Bridge - Junction of Hertford Union Canal - Regent's Canal - Old Ford Lock - Acton's Lock - Kingsland Basin - Sturts Lock - City Road Basin - Eastern end of Islington Tunnel - Angel Underground Station.

Map - O.S. 1:25,000 Explorer Series No. - 173 - London North.

Start - Limehouse Station, DLR/Limehouse Basin.
End - The Angel Underground Station.

Inns - The New Globe, Mile End. The Palm Tree Inn, Globe Town. Narrow Boat Inn, opposite City Basin.

Cafes - Regent's Canal - Towpath Cafe, near Johnsons Lock/ Mile End Park. Cafe near Acton's Lock.

ABOUT THE WALK - First along the Regent's canal from Limehouse Basin to the junction with the Hertford Union Canal - (see the next walk, a "mini" canal ring walk.) Continuing on along the Regent's Canal to the eastern end of the Islington Tunnel, taking you into the heart of the city. Here you ascend to the Angel Underground Station, or alternatively, continue along the Regent's Canal to Little Venice, as detailed as a separate walk; thus walking the Regents Canal, end to end.

WALKING INSTRUCTIONS - From Limehouse Station, descend to the road and turn right, and right again at the main road - Commercial Road. In a few yards right again and pass under the railway line before turning left to the Limehouse Basin. Keep to the lefthand side and cross a footbridge and turn

15

Locks at the start of the Regent's Canal.

Salmon Lane Lock.

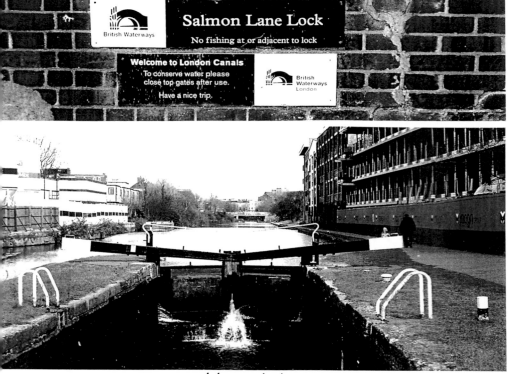

Johnsons Lock.

left past locks and the start of the Regent's Canal. For the next two miles keep the canal on your left to the junction with the Hertford Union Canal on the right. First pass Salmon Lock on the left and 3/4 mile later reach Johnsons Lock with Mile End Park on the right. In 1/2 mile gain Mile End Lock and a further 1/2 mile pass The Palm Tree Inn. 1/4 mile later you are at the bridge and the junction of the Herford Union Canal - Lee Valley Park 1 1/4 miles.

Continuing to the Islington Tunnel, keep straight ahead with the Regent's Canal on your left and pass Old Ford Lock, almost immediately. Continue beside the canal for the next two miles, passing Victoria Park on the right and Acton's Lock in a mile. In 3/4 mile pass Kingsland Basin, built in 1830, on the right. In almost a mile gain Sturts Lock and 1/2 mile later the City Basin and City Road Lock, before Islington Tunnel. At the tunnel entrance ascend to the road. Keep straight ahead to the York Inn and main shopping area of Islington. Turn left to the Angel Underground Station. The first part from the tunnel you are following the line of the tunnel as no towpath was made. The route is signed on the ground with circular discs and blue rippled discs set into the pavement.

LIMEHOUSE BASIN - Opened in 1820 and originally known as the Regent's Canal Dock. The basin was once a thriving inland port and at one stage there were so many boats that it was possible to walk from one to another across the basin. Exotic csrgo was unloaded here and placed into canal boats for delivery nationwide. Later the main cargo was coal from the northern collieries. Trade ceased in 1969.

VICTORIA PARK - Built between 1842-45 and designed by James Pennelthorne, becoming the World's first public park. Queen Victoria, after which it is named, did not visit the park until 1873.

HERTFORD UNION CANAL - 1 1/4 miles long and completed in 1830 with three locks to the River Lee Navigation. Often known as Duckett's Cut, as the builder was Sir George Duckett, the proprietor of the River Stort Navigation - see my separate book on this navigation. This short canal provided a shorter route to the Grand Union Canal and central London, than going via the Limehouse Basin.

ISLINGTON TUNNEL - 960 yards / 878 metres long. Took three years to build between 1815-1818. There is no towpath; the horse were led over the top while the narrow boats were legged through.

Kingsland Basin.

Sturts Lock.

CITY ROAD BASIN - Built in 1820 and once covered four acres. Pickford's, the Removers, had a base here.

REGENT'S CANAL, HERTFORD UNION CANAL and RIVER LEE NAVIGATION - 6 MILES

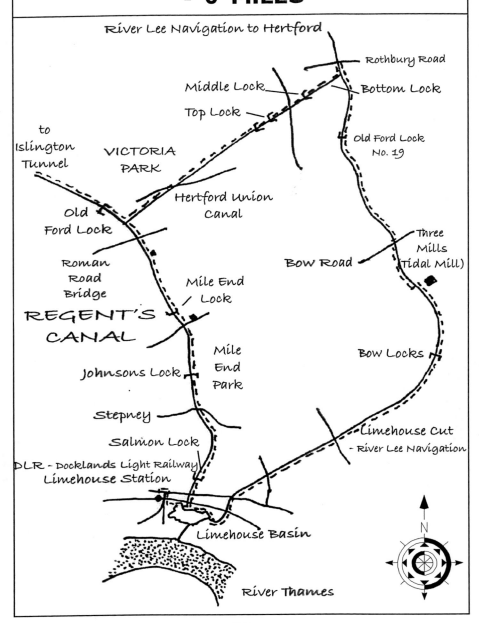

River Lee Navigation to Hertford

Rothbury Road

Middle Lock

Bottom Lock

Top Lock

Old Ford Lock No. 19

to Islington Tunnel

VICTORIA PARK

Hertford Union Canal

Old Ford Lock

Three Mills (Tidal Mill)

Roman Road Bridge

Bow Road

REGENT'S CANAL

Mile End Lock

Johnsons Lock

Mile End Park

Bow Locks

Stepney

Salmon Lock

Limehouse Cut - River Lee Navigation

DLR - Docklands Light Railway Limehouse Station

Limehouse Basin

N

River Thames

REGENT'S CANAL , THE HERTFORD UNION CANAL AND RIVER LEE NAVIGATION, - 6 miles - allow 3 hours.

Basic route - Limehouse Basin - Regent's Canal - Mile End Park - Roman Road Bridge - Hertford Union Canal - River Lee Navigation - Old Ford Lock No. 19 - Mill House, Tidal Mill - Bow Locks - Limehouse Cut - Limehouse Basin.

Map - O.S. 1:25,000 Explorer Series Nos. - 173 - London North, covers all the route except for Mill House and Bow Locks; those are on Map No. 162.

Start and end - Limehouse Station, DLR/Limehouse Basin.

Inns - The New Globe, Mile End. The Palm Tree Inn, Globe Town.

Cafes - Regent's Canal - Towpath Cafe, near Johnsons Lock/ Mile End Park. River Lee Navigation - McDonald's, Bow Flyover.

ABOUT THE WALK - The main walk is a delightful canal ring; perhaps the smallest in Britain? First along the Regent's canal from Limehouse Basin to the Hertford Union Canal. Down that to the River Lee Navigation. Turning right you walk past the Clock House Mill,a tidal Mill, onto Bow Locks and the Limehouse Cut back to the Limehouse Basin. You are assured a rewarding city canal walk, past locks and basins rich in history.

WALKING INSTRUCTIONS - From Limehouse Station, descend to the road and turn right, and right again at the main road - Commercial Road. In a few yards right again and pass under the railway line before turning left to the Limehouse Basin. Keep to the lefthand side and cross a footbridge and turn left past locks and the start of the Regent's Canal. For the next two miles keep the canal on your left to the junction with the Hertford Union Canal on the right. First pass Salmon Lane Lock on the left and 3/4 mile later reach Johnsons Lock with Mile End Park on the right. In 1/2 mile gain Mile End Lock and a further 1/2 mile pass The Palm Tree Inn. 1/4 mile later you are at the bridge and junction of the Herford Union Canal - path signed - Lee Valley Park 1 1/4 miles. Turn right here to continue the canal ring.

Follow the towpath on the lefthand side of the Hertford Union Canal and in a mile reach Top Lock, then Middle Lock and finally Bottom Lock before the River Lee Navigation. Turn left to the bridge - White Post Lane - and cross over and turn right down to the towpath. Keep beside the Navigation on your right, at first, all the way back to Limehouse Basin, 2 1/2 miles away. In a mile reach the Bow Flyover, just after Bow Back River. Cross with care - McDonald's is to your right. Walk down past a calor gas bottle store back to the navigation, which is now on your left. In 1/4 mile cross to Mill House, a Tidal Mill, (Three Mills) and now for the rest of the walk the navigation is on your right. 1/4 mile later cross the white bridge over Bow Locks No. 20 and walk along the Limehouse Cut back to Limehouse Basin 1 1/2 miles away. Reaching the basin, turn right to the start of the Regent's Canal and left to retrace you steps back over the bridge and onto Limehouse Station. If wanting explore the basin and see the River Thames, turn left to the lock and onto the river. Continue walking clockwise around the basin to rejoin your starting out path.

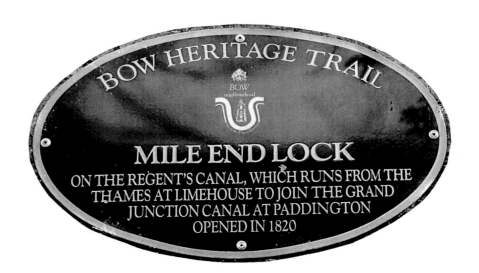

Mile End Lock.

Three Mills - Tidal Mills.
The timbered framed House Mill was built in 1776 and is the largest
tidal Mill in Britain with four undershot waterwheels. The Clock Mill
with Clock House and Oast towers dates from 1750.

REGENT'S CANAL - ISLINGTON TUNNEL TO LITTLE VENICE - 4 1/2 MILES

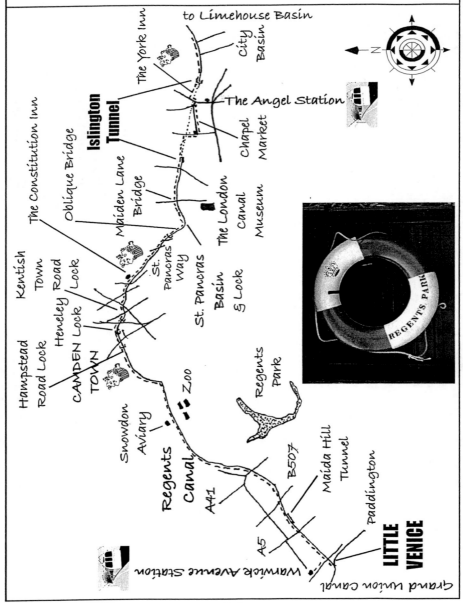

to Limehouse Basin

The York Inn

City Basin

The Angel Station

Islington Tunnel

Chapel Market

The Constitution Inn

Oblique Bridge

Maiden Lane Bridge

The London Canal Museum

Kentish Town

Henley Road Lock

St. Pancras Way

St. Pancras Basin & Lock

Hampstead Road Lock

CAMDEN Lock Lock TOWN

Regents Park

REGENTS PARK

Snowdon Aviary

Zoo

Regents Park

Regents Canal

Maida Hill Tunnel

Paddington

A41

B507

A5

Warwick Avenue Station

LITTLE VENICE

Grand Union Canal

*Basic route - **Angel Underground** Station - **Islington** Tunnel (Eastern end) - **Chapel** Market - Maygood Street - **Western** End - Regent's **Canal** - Battlebridge Basin - Kings **Cross** - St. Pancras Basin - **Kentish** Town Road Lock - **Hawley** Lock - Camden Town/Lock - Hampstead Road Lock - **cumberland** Basin - Regents Zoo – Snowdon Aviary - Regents **park** – Maida Hill Tunnel - Aberdeen Place - Junction House - **Little** Venice - Warwick Avenue **Underground** Station.*

*Map - O.S. 1:25,000 **Explorer** Series No. 173 - **North London**.*

*Start - Angel **Underground** Station - Northern **Line**.
End - Warwick **Avenue** Underground Station - **Bakerloo** Line.*

*Inns - Salmon & **Compass**, Chapel Market. The **Constitution** Inn, St. Pancras **Way**. Several at Camden **Market**.*

*Teas - Chapel **Market**. Camden Market.*

ABOUT THE WALK - The Western half of the canal past Kings Cross and St. Pancras and onto Camden Locks and adjacent market; which is well worth visiting. Then the canal become quieter as it passes around Regent's Park and the final mile to Little Venice via the Maida Hill Tunnel. At Little Venice you have reached the Paddington Branch of the Grand Union Canal and completed the end to end walk and Regent's Canal. Here you can either turn right to Warwick Avenue Underground Station or make it a circular walk by walking to Paddington Basin and onto Hyde Park - 8 miles (12 overall) - see the next walk details.

WALKING INSTRUCTIONS - From the underground turn right then left across the crossing into Liverpool Street. In a few yards turn left along Chapel

British Waterways London

Legging the longest tunnel

At 960 yards (878 metres) long, the Islington Tunnel is James Morgan's greatest engineering achievement. For early boaters, getting through it was an achievement as well there was no towpath so they couldn't use their horses.

To 'leg' a boat through, two boaters lay on their backs on planks laid across the bows. Then they 'walked' along the sides of the tunnel, inching the boat forwards with their feet.

Getting through the tunnel was also an achievement for early boaters, as there was no towpath. This meant they couldn't use their horses.

Two men legging a boat through the tunnel

Heritage Lottery Fund

THE REGENT'S CANAL

There are several historical plaques along the Regent's Canal and this tells you about the Islington Tunnel.

26

Market -a busy market. The whole route is signed on the ground with circular discs - keep to the lefthand side to follow them along Chapel Market. At the end turn right by the Salmon and Compass Inn and take the second road on your left - Maygood Street. Keep straight ahead through a housing estate, as marked on the ground and reaching a small lawn area keep right to the road, with the canal just ahead. Descend steps to the canal close to the western end of the Islington Tunnel.

Follow the towpath with the canal on your left. In 150 yards at your first road bridge you can turn right and cross the bridge - Caledonian Road, then right again along All Saints Street, to reach the London Canal Museum beside the Battlebridge Basin. Continue along the canal passing the basin on your left then under Maiden Lane Bridge. Kings Cross and St. Pancras are on your left, as the canal swings right to St. Pancras Lock and canal basin on the left. Continue on the towpath under Oblique Bridge and 1/2 mile later reach The Constitution Inn and St. Pancras Way. The sign here states - Camden Lock 1/2 mile; Little Venice 2 3/4 miles.

St. Pancras Lock.

*St. Pancras Way and The **Constitution** Inn.*

Two bridges later - Camden Road - has rope grooves on a metal post. Pass Kentish Town Road Lock and soon after Hawley Lock. The on your right is Camden Market and the towpath merges with the market before you pass Hampstead Road Lock. Less than 1/2 mile later the canal turns sharp right, with Cumberland Basin on your left with an impressive Chinese Restaurant on a former barge - Feng Shang. You are now beside Regent's Park on your left and no doubt seeing some wolves on the left and passing the Snowdon Aviary on the right.

Camden Road bridge and rope grooves.

29

Hampstead Road Lock, Camden Town.

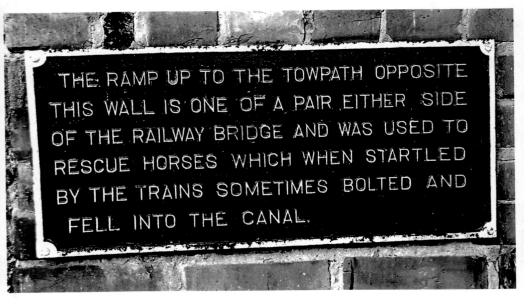

THE RAMP UP TO THE TOWPATH OPPOSITE THIS WALL IS ONE OF A PAIR EITHER SIDE OF THE RAILWAY BRIDGE AND WAS USED TO RESCUE HORSES WHICH WHEN STARTLED BY THE TRAINS SOMETIMES BOLTED AND FELL INTO THE CANAL.

Historic plaque beyond Camden.

30

Cumberland Basin and the Chinese Restaurant - Feng Shang.

Macclesfield Bridge, Regent's Park - more recent bridge on its original cast iron pillars. The original was hit by a boat in 1874 with explosives and blew up, killing three workers.

Lisson Grove Bridge.

A mile later pass moorings and walk **through** a small tunnel bridge - **Lisson Grove Bridge** - before gaining Maida **Hill Tunn**el. This has no towpath and **you** have **to** ascend steps. At the top turn left **then** right and keep straight **ahead** to **Aberde**en Place and regain the **canal by** a restaurant over the **tunnel** entrance. You have to road walk here, **beside** the canal with moorings **on** your **left.** Before the next bridge turn left **down** onto the towpath past Junction House **(for**mer canal toll house) and **gain** Little Venice. To your right **is the** start **of the** Paddington Branch of the **Grand** Union Canal and on your left **the** small **stret**ch of canal to Paddington Basin. Gain the bridge by Junction **House** and **turn ri**ght along the road to Warwick Avenue Underground.

*Maida **Hill** Tunnel - 272 yards long - you can see the other end. No towpath,
you ascend the steps on the right to reach the other end and Little Venice.*

Little Venice.

33

LONDON CANAL MUSEUM - 12-13, New Wharf Road, London. N1 9RT. Open Tuesday to Sunday - 10.0 a.m. to 4.30 p.m. Here on two floors you can explore the history of the Regent's Canal and British Canals; and walk into a canal barge to see how they lived. The Museum is in a former ice warehouse built in 1863, by Carlo Gatti to store ice; he was also a famous ice-cream maker. Here ice was brought by boat from Scandinavia and sold.

BATTLEBRIDGE BASIN - So named as it is believed Queen Boudicea fought the Romans here in AD61. It was built in 1820 for William Horsfall and for a while was known as Horsfall Basin.

The London Canal Museum can be seen just left of centre.

LITTLE VENICE VIA RIVER THAMES
TO ISLINGTON TUNNEL - 8 MILES

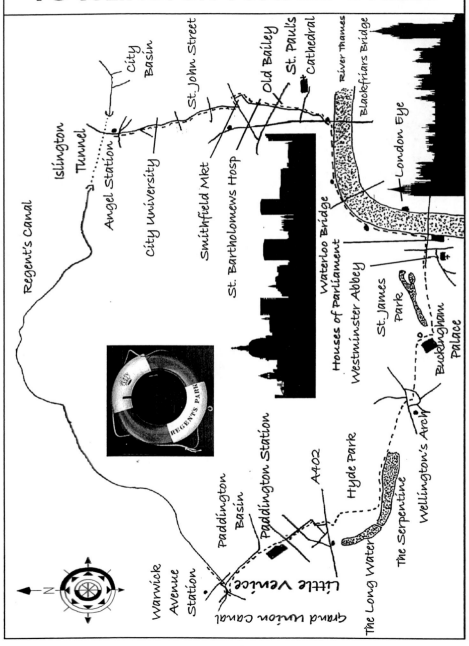

City Basin

Islington Tunnel

St. John Street

Old Bailey

St. Paul's Cathedral

River Thames

Blackfriars Bridge

Angel Station

City University

London Eye

Smithfield Mkt

Regent's Canal

St. Bartholomews Hosp

Waterloo Bridge

Houses of Parliament

Westminster Abbey

St. James Park

Buckingham Palace

Paddington Basin

Paddington Station

A402

Hyde Park

Wellington's Arch

The Serpentine

The Long Water

Warwick Avenue Station

Little Venice

Grand Union Canal

REGENT'S PARK

N

LITTLE VENICE VIA RIVER THAMES TO ISLINGTON TUNNEL
- 8 MILES
- allow 4 to 5 hours.

Basic route - Little Venice/Paddington Branch of the Grand Union Canal - Paddington Station - Lancaster Gate - Hyde Park - The Serpentine - Wellington's Arch - Buckingham Palace - St. James Park - Parliament Square - Westminster Bridge - Thames Path - Embankment - Waterloo Bridge - Blackfriars Bridge - St. Paul's Cathedral - The Angel Underground Station, Islington.

Map - O.S. 1:25,000 Explorer Series No. 173 - London North.

Start - Warwick Avenue Underground Station (Bakerloo Line) - Little Venice.
End - The Angel Underground Station (Northern Line) - Islington Tunnel.

Inns - Numerous along the route.

Cafe - Numerous along the route, including Hyde Park.

ABOUT THE WALK - Primarily this is a part of a circular walk from Islington Tunnel, along the Regent's canal to Little Venice and on into Hyde Park, past Buckingham Palace and Big Ben to the River Thames. A two mile walk along here to Blackfriars Bridge brings you to the last segment as you pass near St. Paul's and return to the Angel, Islington. The whole circular walk is approximately 13 miles long. By doing this circuit you to see at one fell swoop many of the principal places in English history. With so much to see it could be a very long day! You pass numerous underground stations from Paddington onwards so you can always stop and return another day to complete the route. Whatever you do it you are assured a level but remarkable walk in London's fair city!

WALKING INSTRUCTIONS - From Little Venice at Junction House, follow the towpath round to your right past the Puppet Theatre to the next bridge. Ascend to it and cross and descend the other side back to Little Venice Basin. Follow the canal arm right towards Paddington, passing the Waterbus terminus and floating cafe/restaurant's. In 1/2 mile the canal arm turns left to Paddington Basin and its end. Here leave the canal and keep straight ahead, as signed for Paddington Station. You soon reach a road - London Street - keeping straight ahead along it, passing a Royal mail sorting office on your left, to a road with Paddington Station on your right. Cross and continue along London Street. Pass Norfolk Square on your left, then Surrey Place and Gloucester Square - you are now in Bayswater Road. Where the main road turns left opposite The Victoria Inn, turn right into Stanhope Terrace. Take the first road on your left - Brook Street - and keep straight ahead along it to the A402 and Victoria Gate on the edge of Hyde Park. (To your right is Lancaster Gate Underground Station).

Wellington's Arch.

Cross into the park and keep straight ahead on the tarmaced path beside a park road on your right - path signed The Serpentine. Follow it all the way to a parking area and The Serpentine. Turn left and follow the path close to the lake. In 1/2 mile at the end of the Serpentine and Dell Cafe, keep straight ahead on the tarmaced path to Hyde Park Corner (Underground Station to your right). Cross the road following the wide path and pass under Wellington's Arch to the next road. Cross and keep to the lefthand side of Constitution Hill to Buckingham Palace.

Embankment and Cleopatra's Needle.

Turn right past the Palace gates and then left along Birdcage Walk, with St. James Park on your left and The Guards Museum on your right. Keep straight ahead into Parliament Square with Westminster Abbey to your right. Continue ahead to the Houses of Parliament, Big Ben and the River Thames. (Westminster Underground Station on your left.) At Westminster Bridge turn left along the embankment with the London Eye on the otherside of the river. In 1/2 mile pass Embankment Underground Station on your left. Continue ahead beside the Thames on the Thames Path (Victoria Embankment) and pass Cleopatra's Needle and Waterloo Bridge. 1/4 mile later, Temple Underground Station on your left and the City of London marker statue. Pass the boats DHOS Wellington and HMS President before nearing Blackfriars Bridge. Here you leave the Thames and cross the road to walk past the Unilever Building on the left with Blackfriars Underground Station on your right. The next section is full of history with plaques, statues and information boards.

39

River Thames, London Eye, and Big Ben.

Continue and cross the road to the Black Friars Inn. Turn right beside it and then left along Black Friars Lane - path signed to St. Paul's. Keep straight ahead along the narrow lane past the Apothecaries Hall to Pilgrim's Street. Cross, still keeping straight ahead, to Ludgate Hill with St. Paul's Cathedral to your right, and St. Martin's - a Wren church. Go straight across into Old Bailey and soon pass on the right the famous Central Criminal Court.

Keep straight ahead and cross the A50 with the church St. Sepulchre with Newgate on the left and The Viaduct Tavern on the right. Walk along Gilchrist Street with Merrill Lynch (no relation!) on the right. Pass Pye Corner and the Golden Boy statue on the left (Great Fire of London, 1666) and St. Bartholomew's Hospital on the right. At the top keep right around the circle and pass Sir William Wallace monument, who was hung, drawn and quartered near here on August 23rd. 1305. Walk through Central Avenue of Springfield Market.

Continue straight ahead for the final 1 1/4 miles, most of the time along the aptly named, St. John Street. Cross Clerkenwell Road and at the next road. pass the Peasant Inn, still on St. John Street. Next, pass City University on your right and soon afterwards to your left is Sadlers Wells Theatre. You are now on Islington High Street and in 1/4 mile on the right is the Angel Underground Station, where you began.

*Boundary marker of The **City of Lond**on.*

THE GRAND UNION CANAL
- Some brief history notes.

King George III in April 1793, gave his assent to an Act of Parliament -

"For making and maintaining a Navigable Canal from Braunston in the County of Northamptonshire to join the River Thames at or near Brentford in the County of Middlesex."

Originally known as the Grand Junction Canal, work began in 1793 with William Jessop of Derbyshire as the Chief Engineer and James Barnes saw to most of the construction work. The most famous section - the Hanwell Flight of six locks - near Brentford was completed in 1794 and raised the canal 53 ft. in 1/3 mile. This flight and the nearby Three Bridges - where the road, canal and railway exactly cross, are now Scheduled Ancient Monuments.

Although sections were opened from 1796 onwards, it wasn't until August 1805 when the canal from Braunston to the River Thames was completely opened. In the meantime the Paddington Branch, from Bull's Bridge to Paddington Basin - 400 yards long by 30 yards wide - was opened on 10th. July 1801. This was a major boost to trade as until then goods were carried on the Thames to the city. There was also a passenger boat service - The Paddington Packet Boat - that ran from Paddington to Uxbridge, and was a great success for many years.

As with all canals the railways brought a decline in use and from the mid 19th. century it was a battle to survive. The Grand Junction fared better than most as it brought goods to and from London. By the 1920's plans were afoot to merge the Warwick, Regent and Grand Junction Canals together and combined they could carry on and make improvements. An Act of Parliament in 1928 allowed the merger to take place on January 1st. 1929. The Regent Canal Company bought the two other canals companies for £801,442. 13p. and the company became known as the Grand Union Canal. New narrow boats were designed which proved a success and run by the Grand Union Canal Carrying Company. In 1948 the canals were nationalised and the Grand Union Canal was one of the last to cease commercial traffic.

As you walk the canal you will see the locks are numbered (not on the Paddington Arm, as there aren't anyway) and the bridges are named and numbered from Little Venice. There are a few Braunston mile posts scattered around and each London Borough has its own marker.

Acton Lane, Harlesden, Bridge plaque.

Canal Bridge with rope grooves and historic Grand Juntion Canal Co. 1909, support bosses, opposite Horsenden Hill/Perival Wood.

THE GRAND UNION CANAL - PADDINGTON BRANCH - LITTLE VENICE TO ALPERTON - 6 1/2 MILES

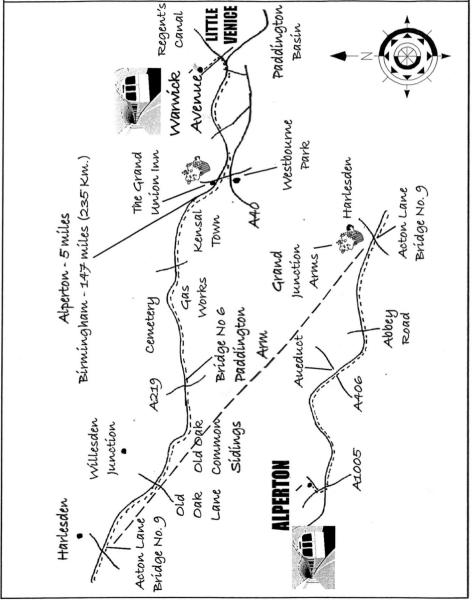

Regent's Canal

LITTLE VENICE

Paddington Basin

Warwick Avenue

Westbourne Park

The Grand Union Inn

Alperton - 5 miles
Birmingham - 147 miles (235 Km.)

Kensal Town

A40

Grand Junction Arms

Harlesden

Acton Lane Bridge No. 9

Gas Works

Cemetery

A219

Bridge No 6

Paddington Arm

Aqueduct

Abbey Road

A406

Willesden Junction

Old Oak Lane

Old Oak Common Sidings

A1005

ALPERTON

Harlesden

Acton Lane Bridge No. 9

THE GRAND UNION CANAL - PADDINGTON BRANCH - LITTLE VENICE TO ALPERTON - 6 1/2 MILES - allow 3 hours.

Basic route - Warwick Avenue Underground Station - Little Venice - Paddington Branch of the Grand Union Canal - The Grand Union Inn - Kensal Town - Halfpenny Bridge - Kensal Green Moorings - Gas Works – Bridge No. 6 (A219) - Old Oak Common Sidings - Grand Junction Arms - A406 Aqueduct - Ealing Road Bridge (A4005) - Alperton Underground Station.

Map - O.S. 1:25,000 Explorer Series No. 173 - London North.

Start - Warwick Avenue Underground Station (Little Venice). End - Alperton Underground Station.

Inns - The Grand Union (Westbourne Green). Grand Junction Arms, Acton Lane Bridge No. 9. The Pleasure Boat Inn, Ealing Road.

Cafe - Boat cafe at Little Venice. Abbey Pont Cafe, Abbey Road (Park Royal).

ABOUT THE WALK - Level walking along almost half of the Paddington Branch of the Grand Union Canal. No locks on this section but one aqueduct over the A406. Very pleasant walking and surprisingly attractive as you walk westwards from the city of London. The walk starts and ends at underground stations.

WALKING INSTRUCTIONS - From Warwick Avenue Station walk out following the signs for Little Venice. Turn right and soon left over Westbourne Terrace Bridge and turn left down to a cafe boat and the canal. Turn left   -

The Grand Union Inn.

path signed **Ladygrove** and Kensal Green - and **walk under the** bridge. You keep the canal **on your** right the whole way to **Alperton. Pass the** Little Venice Moorings and **in a mile** pass the aptly named, The **Grand Union** Inn. Here the path sign states, **Paddington** 1 mile / Alperton 5 **miles. These** signs you pass frequently as **your walk** along. Almost immediately **is another sign** - Birmingham 147 miles (235 km); the whole of the canal to **the Midlands!** Continue on past gardens **and Kensal** Town and the former **halfpenny bridge** on the right. 1/2 mile later **Sainsbury**'s on the left and a rowing **activities centre** on the left, before crossing **bridges** to a delightful quiet **section of the canal**, just after Kensal Green **Moorings**. On your left is a gas **works and on the** right a large cemetery. Part **way** along are picnic tables.

A mile later **reach** Bridge No. 6 of the **Paddington Arm; the** bridges are numbered from **Little** Venice. Alperton is now 3 1/4 **miles - you are** halfway! Next pass Old **Oak** Common Sidings on your **left before reaching** Old Oak Lane Bridge (**A407**). 3/4 mile later gain Acton **Lane Bridge No.** 9, with the Grand Junction **Arms** on the right. A path sign states **the end of the** Paddington Arm at Bull's **Bridge is** 9 miles - the next walk! **Continue, now past** industrial complexes to **Abbey** Road bridge and cafe - **Abbey Point Cafe**; Alperton 2 miles. Just after **the** canal curves right and crosses **the A406** by a splendid

3 1/4 miles to Alberton.

Acton Lane Bridge No. 9 - Grand Junction Arms.

aqueduct. To your left is the Wembley Travelodge and to the right Wembley Stadium.

A406 Aqueduct.

Continue on the towpath is it now turns left then right to Alperton. You pass under the Piccadilly line before leaving the canal at Ealing Road at Alperton. Cross to your right with the Pleasure Boat Inn on your left. Turn right along Ealing Road to Alperton Tube Station on the left.

ALPERTON, GRAND UNION CANAL AND BRENT RIVER
- 17 MILES - MAP ONE

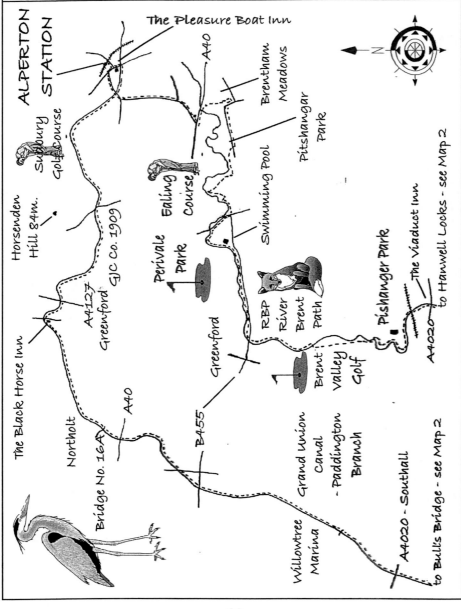

The Pleasure Boat Inn

ALPERTON STATION

Sudbury Golf Course

A40

Brentham Meadows

Pitshangar Park

Horsenden Hill 84m.

A4127 Greenford GJC Co. 1909

Ealing Golf Course

Swimming Pool

The Viaduct Inn

to Hanwell Locks - see Map 2

The Black Horse Inn

Perivale Park

RBP River Brent Path

Pishanger Park

A4020

Greenford

Brent Valley Golf

Northolt

A40

Bridge No. 16A

B455

Grand Union Canal - Paddington Branch

A4020 - Southall

Willowtree Marina

to Bull's Bridge - see Map 2

N

48

PADDINGTON BRANCH, GRAND UNION CANAL AND BRENT RIVER PARK
- 17 MILES
- allow 6 to 7 hours.

*Basic route - **Alperton** - Grand Union **Canal** (Paddington Branch) - Horsenden Hill - Northolt - **Southall** – Bull's Bridge - Grand **Union Canal** - Hanwell Locks - **River** Brent Park Walk - Pishanger Park - Greenford - **Perivale Park** - Ealing Golf Course - **Brentham** Meadows - A40 – Alperton.*

Map - O.S. 1:25,000 Explorer Series No. 173 – London North.

Start and end - Alperton Underground Station (Piccadilly Line).

*Inns - The **Pleasure** Boat Inn, Alperton. The **Black Horse**, Greenford. The Civil Engineer, **Northolt**. Hamborough Tavern, **Southall**. **Grand** Junction Arms, **Hyde**. The Old Oak Tree Inn and The Lamb Inn, North Hyde. The **Viaduct**, Hanwell. The **Lightning**, Alperton Lane.*

*Refreshments - Pishanger Park, Brent **River Park** - just off the route.*

ABOUT THE WALK - One of the longest in the book! However, it is perhaps the best! Apart from a little road walking at the end, you are beside a canal or river for 16 miles. The first seven miles are beside the Paddington Branch of the Grand Union Canal to its junction with the main Grand Union Canal at Bull's Bridge near Hillingdon. Heading east you walk beside the canal for three miles to the famous Hanwell flight of locks - a highlight of the walk. Here you leave the canal to follow the signed River Brent Park walk northwards, for about six miles, back to near Alperton. A short road walk

49

returns you to Alperton Station. A long but rewarding day in west London. There is plenty of wildfowl on the canal and at one stage I thought I was in the jungle with green parrots flying above, grey heron's on the bankside and a lone red fox asleep in the rushes – this why I walk!

WALKING INSTRUCTIONS - From Alperton Station, turn right down Ealing Road to the A404 road (Bridgewater Road), opposite the Pleasure Boat Inn. Cross the road and turn left over the bridge and right immediately down to the towpath. You now follow this, with the canal on your right, for seven miles (2 1/2 hours) to Bull's Bridge and canal junction. First pass under Bridge No. 12 - Manor Farm Road, which you will walk over at the end. Bull's Bridge is 7 miles, as signed. Pass a cemetery on the right before the canal turns left passing Sudbury Golf Course on the right. Later pass Willowtree Boat Trips and Horsenden Hill on the right, before the next bridge. This has some fine rope groves and metal plates supporting the bridge with the former canal's owners name On - GJC Co. 1909. - (Grand Junction Canal Co 1909). Almost a mile later and before the next bridge - A4127 - on your left is a rare canal mile post - 5 miles to Bull's Bridge.

Bridge with metal plates - GJC Co. 1909 & rope grooves.

THE BLACK HORSE

1/4 mile later pass **under** another bridge **which gives** access to Greenford Station, 1/4 mile south. On the left is **The Black** Horse Inn. Pass Greenford **Visitor's** Moorings area and just **after cross** a bridge over the **entrance to a** small basin on your left. **A mile later** pass an industrial area **and a mosque** before bridge No. 16A **before** passing under the **A40 road.** The canal is now heading **southwards** and soon pass a wooden **bridge** with Green Man carvings. **Two bridges** later, (B455), **to the right is** the Civil Engineer Inn. **In another** 1/2 mile pass a marina **on your right** and just after on **the left is a** Canal Way plaque - **Ealing, Borough** of London.

Almost a mile later on **your right is** Willowtree Marina **and on the** left Spikes Bridge Park. Pass another **footbridge** and Hillingdon Trail **signs.** Here too is another Canal Way sign - London **Borough** of Hillingdon. **1/2 mile** later pass under the A4020 with the **Hamborough** Tavern on the **left.** Pass Uxbridge

ALPERTON, GRAND UNION CANAL AND BRENT RIVER
- 17 MILES - MAP TWO

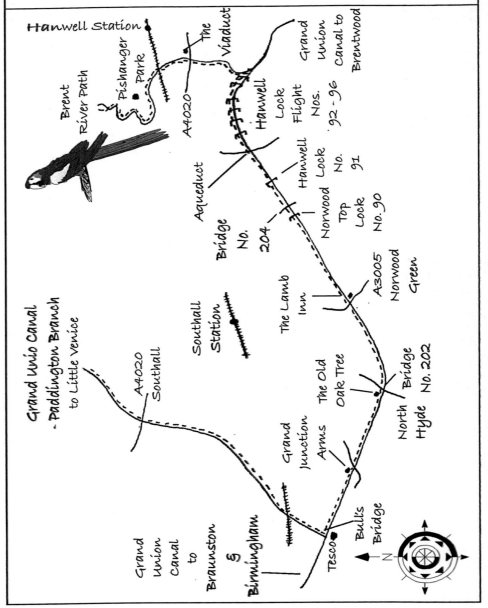

Hanwell Station

Brent River Path

Pishanger Park

A4020

The Viaduct

Hanwell Lock Flight Nos. 92 - 96

Grand Union Canal to Brentwood

Hanwell Lock No. 91

Norwood Top Lock No. 90

Aqueduct

Bridge No. 204

The Lamb Inn

A3005 Norwood Green

Southall Station

Grand Unio Canal - Paddington Branch to Little Venice

A4020 Southall

The Old Oak Tree

North Hyde Bridge No. 202

Grand Junction Arms

Grand Union Canal to Braunston & Birmingham

Tesco

Bull's Bridge

N

Road Moorings and path sign - Footpath leading to Hayes. You are also on the Hillingdon Trail at this point along the towpath. In another mile pass under a railway line and reach the white painted **Bull's Bridge** and canal junction. This is the end of the Paddington Arm of the **Grand Union** Canal - a thirteen mile stretch of canal without a lock. To your right is the towpath to Birmingham; about 140 miles!

Bull's Bridge and signs.

Turn left and now on the main Grand Union Canal to the River Thames, Brentwood. First on your right are some houseboats and in 1/2 mile the Grand Junction Arms. Afterwards for 1/2 mile the road and houses of Heathway keep you company, before passing Southall Recreation Ground on your left. Pass the Old Oak Tree Inn and a winding hole on the right, before Bridge No. 202 (Regina Road), with rope grooves. in a further 1/2 mile cross a bridge and entrance to a BWB Basin on the left. 1/4 mile later is the A3005 road bridge and Lamb Inn. Just after is a historic canal milepost - GJC Co. 89 miles Braunston. 1/4 mile later pass Boxley Field on the left and then a bridge over a canal arm on your left - although you can't see it.

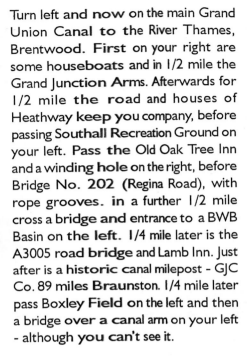

Just after you gain the Hanwell Locks, with Norwood Top Lock No. 90. The next mile of the canal is fascinating walking. Pass bridge no. 204, then Hanwell Lock No. 91 Then cross an aqueduct over the railway line and road - The Three Bridges - before passing four locks in quick succession, part of the Hanwell Flight of Locks. At Lock No. 96 you leave the canal, as signed - Brent River Path. A small path disc with the letters BRP, now guide you for the next six miles.

Norwood Top Lock No. 90.

Now heading north keep the River Brent on your **right and** soon pass under the A4020, again. **You walk** through a small tunnel, **which can** be flooded; if it is you have to ascend **to the** road and cross. To **your right is** the Viaduct Inn. Continue beside the **river to** a railway viaduct and **cross the** footbridge here and turn left, now **with the** river on your left. **The river me**anders here and the path keeps close **to it** as it wriggles it way around **Pishan**ger Park; this is where I saw the **green parrots** - eight of them. **Just past t**he park cross a footbridge over the **river** and turn right. Continue **straight** ahead on a path between the fairways **and** greens of Brent Valley **Golf Course**, and away from the river. After 1/2 **mile** cross a bridge and turn **left, with** a school to your right. The river is **now on** your left for the rest **of the walk**. After 1/4 mile ascend steps near a **weir and** walk above the river; **it was ne**ar here I saw the fox. Pass another **weir and** football field on the **right before** the B455 road - Costons Lane.

Cross the road to the right and rejoin the path which keeps near the river on your left and road on the right. On the otherside of the river is Perivale Park Golf Course. In 3/4 mile pass under a railway line and turn left following the river; on your right is a swimming pool complex. Follow the field edge as you loop round past football fields to Argyle Road. Turn right along it, as signed, to the junction. Turn left as signed - Footpath to Perivale Lane - still on the BRP route. This is a tarmaced path past allotments. Turn left as signed and left again to a footbridge. Don't cross but turn right passing Ealing Golf Course. Turn left to pass tennis courts and into Pishanger Park. Follow the tarmaced path right to the park gates and Meadvale Road. Turn left along the road and right at the end - Neville Road. In a few yards left into Brunswick Road and almost immediately at house no. 5, as path signed turn left to Brentham Meadows, the final piece of Brent River Park.

Keep to the lefthand side of the field to the A40 road. Turn left to reach a gate close to the River Brent. Turn left along the road for a short distance to an underpass on your left. Walk through to the other side and turn right along Alperton Lane. Pass The Lightning Inn and under a railway line and left along Manor Farm Road. Pass a football sports ground - Goals - on your right. At the end of the road, turn right still on Manor Farm Road and cross the Paddington Arm, which you walked at the start. Continue along the road to Bridgewater Road. Turn right and soon after left opposite The Pleasure Boat Inn, along Ealing Road back to Alperton Station.

Hanwell Lock Flight **and Lock** *Keepers Cottage.*

GRAND UNION CANAL, HANWELL FLIGHT, OSTERLEY PARK, SYON HOUSE AND RIVER THAMES - 12 MILES

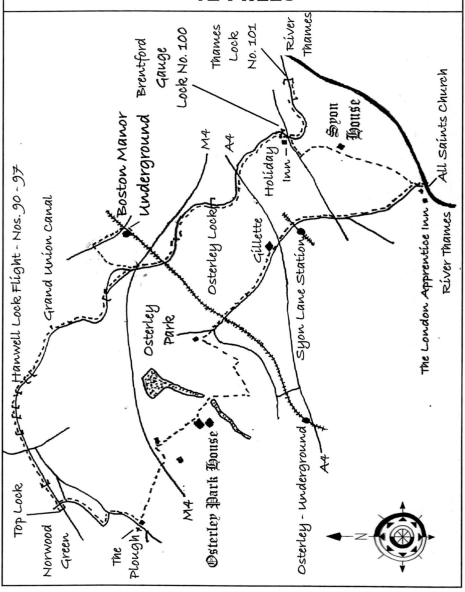

GRAND UNION CANAL, HANWELL FLIGHT, OSTERLEY PARK, SYON HOUSE AND RIVER THAMES
- 12 MILES
- allow 5 hours

Basic route - Boston Manor Underground Station - River Brent - Grand Union Canal - Hanwell Lock Flight nos - 97 - 90 - Top Lock No. 90 - Norwood Green - A4127 - M4 - Osterley Park & House - Wyke Green - B454 - Gillette Building and Corner - Brentford End - A4 - B434 - Park Road - River Thames - Syon Park and House - Grand Union Canal - Thames Lock No. 101 - Grand Union Canal - Clitheroe's Lock No. 99 - River Brent - Boston Manor Underground Station.

Map - O.S. 1:25,000 Explorer Series No. 161 - London South.

Start and end - Boston Manor Underground Station (Piccadilly Line). Alternative starts/end - Osterley Underground (Northern Line). Syon Lane Station, near Gillette Corner.

Inns - The Plough Inn, Norwood Green. The London Apprentice, beside the River Thames, Isleworth - just off the route. George & Dragon Inn, Brentford. The Brogue, Harvester Restaurant, Boston Manor.

Teas - Osterley Park House (Stables). Syon House Garden Centre.

ABOUT THE WALK - A magical mix of canal and lock flight, historic houses and the River Thames. If you visit the houses you will need to add a couple of hours to the route. There is a little road walking in the middle to join Osterley Park and Syon Park, but is quite pleasant as you pass the immaculate Gillette factory, which should be a beacon to how to build a pleasing factory. The two historic parks are most enjoyable and a slight detour brings you to the River

Thames and a historic **church**, near Isleworth. You regain the **canal** at Brentford and you walk down and back along it final length to the **Thames Lock**, before returning and following the canal back to the River Brent and retrace your steps back to Boston **Manor** underground station. If you run out of time, you can always leave the route after Osterley Park (about the 5 mile stage) for Osterley Underground Station. Alternatively in a further 1 1/2 mile is Syon Lane Station (Waterloo - South West Trains). Whatever you do you can be assured of a fascinating full walk in western London, seeing where one of the major canals joins the River Thames.

WALKING INSTRUCTIONS - From Boston Manor Station, turn left along Boston Road (A3002) and in 1/4 mile pass the Harvester Restaurant on your right. Immediately turn left along Royal Gardens - it is path signed River Brent Path and Union Canal. Keep straight ahead to a path gate and follow the path left, soon with the River Brent on your right to the M4 bridge and Grand Union Canal. Turn right; the towpath to your left under the bridge is your return path. Keep the canal on your left for the 2 1/2 miles. First pass Osterley Lock and 1/2 mile later, Platarg Platform works on the left, and then on your right is a historic canal milepost - Braunston 91 miles. Soon after your reach the start of the Hanwell Lock Flight at lock No. 97. You follow them for a mile passing locks No. 96 to 91 with lock keeper's cottages on the left. After 3/4 mile walk beside an aqueduct over the railway line at the three bridges - rail, canal and road above. Little over 1/4 mile later after Lock No. 91 leave the canal at bridge No. 204 infront of Top Lock no. 90 - notice historic plaque - the word Junction has been blacked out.

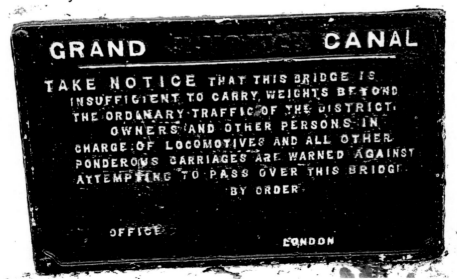

Top Lock No. 90 from Bridge No. 204.

Turn left over the bridge to a road junction; turn right along Melbury Avenue. In 1/4 mile at the next road junction, turn left along Minterne Avenue to the A4127 road, Tentelow Lane. Follow this a short distance to some old houses, at Norwood Green, before the church, (dedicated to St. Mary the Virgin). Before it on the right is the Free School dated 1707. On the left is The Plough Inn. Turn left along its lefthand side as path signed - to St. Mary's Avenue. Keep straight ahead across the road and onto a field, following a defined path across it to steps, gate and path sign before the Osterley Park Road. Turn left and follow it over the M4 and past the entrance to Osterley Park Farm, on the right. Just after reach Avenue Lodge and turn right along the drive to Osterley Park House. In 1/4 mile pass the tea-room on your right and then the impressive house - National Trust property. Follow the tarmaced drive left to pass the lake and onto the car park area. Continue on the drive and shortly after the Farm Shop on the left, turn left to a kissing gate and fenced path. Follow this to another kissing gate, then right then left around the edge of Osterley Park to a Green and South Lodge.

Turn right along the drive to the road junction and keep straight ahead on the B454. Soon pass **Wyke** Green Golf Course Club **House on the left.** 1/2 mile later Grasshoppers **Rugby** pitch. Next it is Tesco's before the impressive Gillette building **and Gillette Corner** at the junction with the A4. Your route is straight across **and use** the subway to continue. Pass **Homebase** on your left and Northumberland Gardens on your right. Pass **Syon Lane Station,** as you follow the road **right (B**434) to the junction with the A314. Go straight across on the A310 road, **following** the signs for Syon House. **In a short** distance the road turns right, **keep left** (straight ahead) along Park Road, passing Isleworth Cemetery on **the right** and the high wall of Syon **Park on your left.**

In 1/2 mile you **reach the** entrance to Syon Park and **House on your** left, but first continue **ahead to** see the River Thames and **the historic** 14th. century tower of All Saints church. Just beyond is the London **Apprentice** Inn. Return to the entrance **gates of** Syon Park and turn right **to follow the** path by the road and now **on a segment** of the Thames Path **(National Trail).** Follow it past the house **(16th. century)** on the right and garden **centre. Continue** ahead to the main **road (A3**14). Turn right past the **George and Dragon** Inn and O'Briers before **the bridge** over the Grand Union **Canal, with a** Holiday Inn on the left - **you will** walk past it shortly. But **first cross the** bridge and immediately **turn right** to follow the towpath beside **the canal.** Pass moored

Thames Lock No. 101 - the end of the Grand Union Canal.

house boats to a no exit sign and ascend steps, to continue beside houses on the left to a road bridge. Turn right through it and regain the towpath past more houses to a footbridge. Cross and continue the final yards with the canal on your left to Thames Lock No. 101, the end of the Grand Union Canal, with the River Thames beyond. Retrace your steps back to the A314 road beside beside the Holiday Inn.

Brentford Gauge Lock No. 100.

Cross to the lefthand side and path sign - Osterley Lock 1 1/2 miles. Keep the canal on your right as you pass the Holiday Inn and Brentford Gauge Lock No. 100. In less than 1/4 mile the towpath leads through a former canal warehouse. Soon after pass under the A4 and the large GSK office block on the right. Soon after pass Clitheroe's Lock No. 99. next pass the canal milepost - Braunston 92 miles - and then cross an impressive metal canal bridge dated 1820 to the otherside. Continue now with the canal on your left. 1/2 mile later pass under the M4 and regain your starting out path. Turn right - path signed Boston Manor Station. Walk beside the River Brent on your left before keeping right where it turns to Royal Gardens. Keep ahead to Boston Road and turn right along it to Boston Manor Station.

Clitheroe's Lock No. 99.

Path waymarkers.

64

Magnificent Canal footpath bridge - Grand Junction Canal Co. 1820.

HANWELL FLIGHT - The six locks here, within a 1/3 rd. of mile, raise the canal 53 feet and are now a Scheduled Ancient Monument. The Three Bridges is an impressive piece of engineering and is the work of Brunel and is also a Scheduled Ancient Monument. Here the railway line, canal (via an aqueduct) and the road cross from different angles.

OSTERLEY HOUSE - The early house was built in 1575 for Sir Thomas Gresham, who created the Royal Exchange. Robert Adam modernised it in 1761 for a wealthy banker family for entertaining his clients and friends. The famed plaster work can be seen at the impressive entrance portico, which you pass. Whilst inside the rooms still astound and impress visitors today for the workmanship. Outside are 18th century gardens and the Stables Tea Room, close to the path. The house and grounds are owned by the National Trust.

ALL SAINTS CHURCH, ISLEWORTH - This is all that remains of the old church, said to have burnt down by two naughty school boys in 1943. You can still see the charred wood in the tower.

SYON HOUSE - Formerly the site was an abbey, named Mt. Zion; an order of Bridgettine nuns. Following the dissolution by Henry 8th. it was rebuilt in today's, somewhat severe style. Since the 18th. century it has been home to the Dukes of Northumberland. Much of the interior is the work of Robert Adam in the 1760's. The grounds are the work of Capability Brown. Today there is a famous Butterfly House, garden centre and an impressive glass house. - the Great Conservatory, built in the 1820's by the 3rd. Duke.

THAMES PATH - 210 mile long National Trail, from its source to the Thames Barrier.

THE RIVER THAMES AND THE "LONDON CANAL LOOP" - 24 miles

The river has been navigable for centuries and to complete the walks in this book, I include a walk from Richmond, back along the Thames to the Limehouse Basin. From here another walk takes you further along the Thames to see the Thames Barrier and back along the Limehouse Cut to Limehouse Basin; thus completing walking around Central London's waterways. I started the River Thames walks from Richmond, on purpose, for you soon pass a Thames Lock and also see what you can't see from the otherside, the channel and lock at the start of the Grand Union Canal. You also see Syon House and much, much more, as you will see in the following walks and pages....Happy walking!

The River Thames, England's premier river, rises at Thames head in the Cotswold Hills and travels 154 miles (248 km) to London Bridge. From here it is a further 56 miles (90 km.) to the open sea. The river is tidal and ebbs and flows to Teddington Lock, some 20 miles inland from London Bridge. Seawards at Woolwich to control the sea surges and to protect London from flooding during the winter months, the Thames Barrier was built in 1982 and stretches 1/3 mile across the Thames; bank to bank.

A National Trail - The Thames Path - follows the banks of the river from its source and the whole route is well signed; see below.

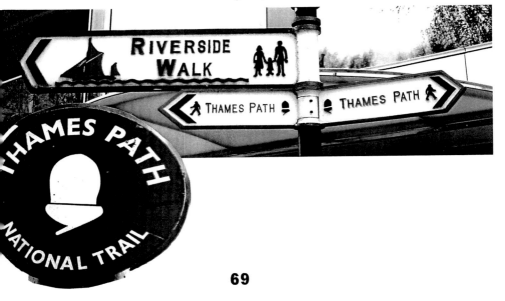

RIVER THAMES - RICHMOND TO WESTMINSTER – 18 MILES
Map One - Richmond to Putney

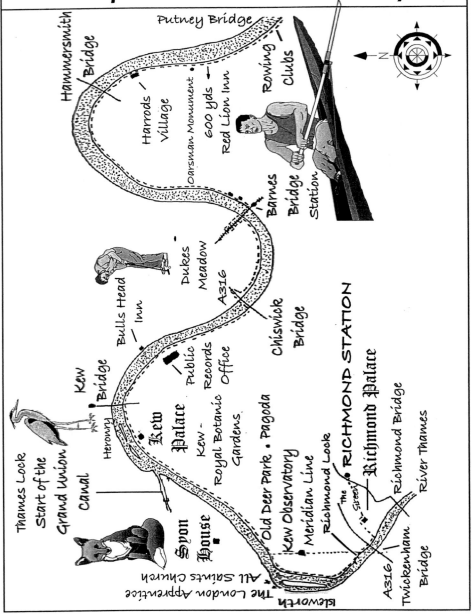

Putney Bridge

Hammersmith Bridge

Rowing Clubs

Harrods Village

600 yds
Red Lion Inn

Oarsman Monument

Barnes Bridge Station

Dukes Meadow

A316

Bulls Head Inn

Chiswick Bridge

Kew Bridge

Public Records Office

Heronry

RICHMOND STATION

Kew Palace

Kew – Royal Botanic Gardens

Richmond Palace

Old Deer Park • Pagoda

Richmond Lock

Richmond Bridge

Kew Observatory

Thames Lock
Start of the
Grand Union Canal

Meridian Line

The Green

River Thames

Spon House

A316
Twickenham Bridge

Isleworth
The London Apprentice
All Saints Church

THE RIVER THAMES - RICHMOND TO WESTMINSTER - 18 MILES - allow 7 hours.

Basic route - Richmond Underground Station - The Green - Richmond Palace - River Thames - Twickenham Bridge - Richmond Lock - Old Deer Park - Kew Gardens - Kew Bridge - Public Records Office - Chiswick Bridge - Barnes Bridge - Hammersmith Bridge - Putney Bridge - Putney - Wandsworth Park - Wandle Creek - Wandsworth Bridge - Battersea Bridge - Albert Bridge - Peace Pagoda - Battersea Park - Chelsea Bridge - Vauxhall Bridge - Lambeth Bridge - Houses of Parliament - Westminster Underground Station.

Map - O.S. 1:25,000 Explorer Series No. 161 - London South.

Start - Richmond Underground Station (District Line).
End - Westminster Underground Station (District & Circle Lines).

Inns - The Cricketers Inn, The Green, Richmond. The Bulls Head, Barnes Bridge. Red Lion Inn, Barnes - 600 yards from path. The Dukes Head, Putney Bridge. The Ship, Wandsworth Bridge. King William I V, Pimlico. Spread Eagle, Millbank.

Cafe's - Putney. McDonald's, Wandsworth Bridge. Battersea Park.

ABOUT THE WALK - This walk has several aims. Firstly you see the end of the Grand Union Canal and Syon House. Secondly you pass several locks and the site of a small canal as you follow the Thames Path. Thirdly the route forms part of a large circular river/canal walk of more than 50 miles, from Limehouse Basin via Regent's canal, Grand Union Canal and River Thames back to Limehouse Basin. Although a long level section - as they all are - there are several underground station close to the route, so you can walk as little or as much as you wish - Stations - Kew Bridge Station, Barnes Bridge Station, Putney Bridge, and Vauxhall Bridge.

The walk itself is stunning and full of history and wildlife. First you pass the remains of the Royal Palace of Richmond, before reaching the River Thames, which is your companion during the walk, The first part is countryside past the Old Deer Park and Kew Gardens - along here I saw many herons and a herony and two red foxes wandering along the waters edge. The path becomes more urban past Kew and Mortlake, although I chose to walk along the northern bank here around Dukes Meadows. After Barnes Bridge the path become "countryside" again to Hammersmith Bridge and past the Wetlands to Putney Bridge. Here you walk inland a bit to get to Wandsworth park - a jewel - before wandering through Wandsworth and back to the Thames in Battersea. After passing Battersea Bridge and Albert Bridge you pass Battersea Park and the Peace Pagoda before crossing the river to the northern side. Now it is all road walking to Westminster.

WALKING INSTRUCTIONS - Gaining the road from Richmond Station, cross to your left, as path signed - Capital Ring - and walk through a passageway on the right of an Estate Agents. Turn left then right to follow the defined path across the Little Green, passing Portland Terrace on the right. At the end reach the former gatehouse of Richmond Palace and a history board. Turn right and then left along the Old Palace Road to Asgill House, the River Thames and Thames path - Thames Path signs and the acorn logo are a constant reminder you are walking the right way! Turn right and soon pass Twickenham Bridge and sign - Kew Bridge 2 3/4 miles. Shortly on your right is the Old Deer park and two Obelisks. These mark with another beyond beside Kew Observatory, the early meridian line; you will pass the northern end in a mile.

Continue to Richmond Lock and 3/4 mile later pass Isleworth and All Saints Church on your left - part of the Osterley-Syon House walk. Soon after pass the northern end of the meridian and the Royal Mid Surrey Golf Course on your right. A stream runs beside the path and is known as the "Mini Ha Ha", after the stately home garden feature. On your left is Syon House. Now for much of the walk rowers (scullers) will be seen practising on the river; you will also pass numerous Rowing Clubs and their boathouses. Continue now with Kew Gardens on your right and a mile later Brentford Dock on your left before the start of the Grand Union Canal. Pass Kew Palace on your right and entrance into the gardens; 1/2 mile later reach Kew Bridge.

Continue along the southern side of the river and in 3/4 mile pass the Public Records Office on your right. Then rowing clubs before Chiswick Bridge. Ascend and cross the bridge and turn right down steps at the end to pass

Richmond Lock.

Syon House from the River Thames.

Tideway Scullers Boathouse, and follow the Thames path along the northern side, around Dukes Meadow. In 3/4 mile as you approach Barnes Bridge (rail bridge), turn left along the road past Chiswick Boathouse and school and cross over and walk right, down the other side of the railway to the river. Ascend steps and cross the footbridge and just before Barnes Bridge Station, descend steps to the road - The Terrace, along the southern side. Pass House No. 9 - Gustave Holst (1874-1934), the composer of The Planet Suite, lived here 1908-1913. Continue past the Bull's Head and soon after leave the road to follow the Thames Path, back into countryside. 1 1/2 mile later reach Hammersmith Bridge.

*The start of the **Grand** Union Canal, from the River **Thames**.*

*Kew Palace, built in 1631, **a** former Royal Palce known as **the Dutch** House.
The Royal Botanical **Gardens** is very well worth visiting **to see the** trees,
gardens and greenhouses.*

74

RIVER THAMES - RICHMOND TO WESTMINSTER - 18 MILES

Map Two - *Putney to Westminster*

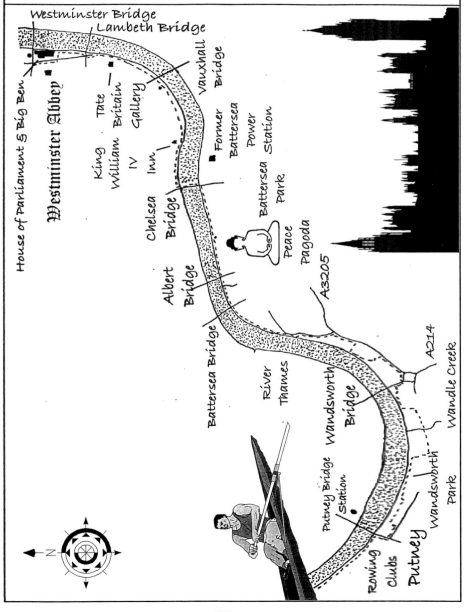

Westminster Bridge
Lambeth Bridge
Vauxhall Bridge
House of Parliament & Big Ben
Westminster Abbey
King William IV
Tate Britain
Gallery
Chelsea Inn
Former Battersea Power Station
Battersea Park
Bridge
Peace Pagoda
Albert Bridge
A3205
Battersea Bridge
River Thames
Wandsworth Bridge
A214
Wandle Creek
Putney Bridge Station
Wandsworth Park
Rowing Clubs
Putney

N

Cross over to continue on the Thames Path and soon pass Harrods Village on your right. A mile from the bridge pass a monument to Steve Fairburn on your right. A little later a path sign on your right indicates that it is 600 yards to the Red lion Inn. Soon after on your left is Fulham Football ground. A little further pass the Beverley Brook Walk on your right and then pass several rowing clubs as you approach Putney Bridge. Here you leave the Thames and turn right passing St. Mary the Virgin church on your left. Head towards Putney shopping area and turn left along Putney Bridge Street. Pass the Abraham Dawes Almshouses, established 1648 and turn left along Deodar Street. Follow it right and at the end keep straight ahead through Blade Mews into Wandsworth Park. Turn left to the riverside and walk along the tree lined path; on the otherside of the river is the white Hurlingham House.

At the end of the park turn right away from the river. Pass an inn and Riverside Quarter on your left. Before the main road and railway, turn left along Osiers Road. Keep ahead along Enterprise Road and over the bridge over Wandle Creek, built May 1999. Continue ahead now along Smugglers Way and turn left as path signed - Waterside path and Riverside Walk/Thames path, by a Refuse area to Nickols Walk and the river. Turn right beside it and before Wandsworth Bridge turn right past the Ship Inn and upto the main road. Turn right to a large roundabout and keep left along the A3205 - a McDonald's is well to your right at the roundabout. In 1/4 mile turn left down Mendip Road back to the Thames, briefly, before leaving it to regain the A3205. Turn left along it and in 1/4 mile left along Lombard Road. After passing under the railway line, in 1/4 mile, turn left to the river. That is the end of river loops and the river/Thames path is now straight forward.

Pass St. Mary's church on the right and opposite is Chelsea Harbour Marina. More than 1/4 mile later reach Battersea Bridge, then cross a lock before Albert Bridge. Now you are in Battersea Park and in more then 1/4 mile pass the Peace Pagoda, with four Buddha Statues on its sides. 1/2 mile later reach Chelsea Bridge and cross over to the northern side of the river. Turn right and soon pass Grosvenor Bridge, then King William IV Inn. Next Dolphin Square and Pimlico Gardens before the Spread Eagle Inn and Vauxhall Bridge. Keep ahead now along Millbank past the Tate Gallery and Millbank Tower to Lambeth Bridge. Here you can leave the pavement and walk through the Victoria Tower Gardens, before exiting at the Houses of Parliament. Continue ahead with Westminster Abbey on your left to Parliament Square and Bridge Street (Westminster Bridge). Turn right to Westminster Underground Station.

The Royal Borough of Kensington & Chelsea

ALBERT BRIDGE
NOTICE

ALL TROOPS
MUST BREAK STEP
WHEN MARCHING
OVER THIS BRIDGE

Albert Bridge.

PEACE PAGODA, Battersea Park - Built by Japanese Buddhist monks as a memorial to Hiroshima.

One of the four Buddha statues in the Peace Pagoda, Battersea Park.

RICHMOND PALACE - Used by Henry 7th and 8th and Elizabeth the First, and was a popular residence with the deer park adjacent. Today only the gatehouse remains, with the Old Court House on the right.

WANDLE CREEK - A medieval Tide Mill existed here and was demolished in 1892. Also now gone is the Feathers Boat House and Inn. A small canal ran nearby, known as McMurray's Canal, which ran from the River Thames to the Surrey Iron Railway. The canal was filled in about 1937.

STEVE FAIRBURN - (1862-1938) - A famous oarsman and coach and the founder of the Head of River Race. The monument is a mile from the start of the University Boat Race Course.

The Victoria Tower Gardens - Palace of Westminster.

RIVER THAMES - WESTMINSTER TO LIMEHOUSE BASIN - 6 MILES

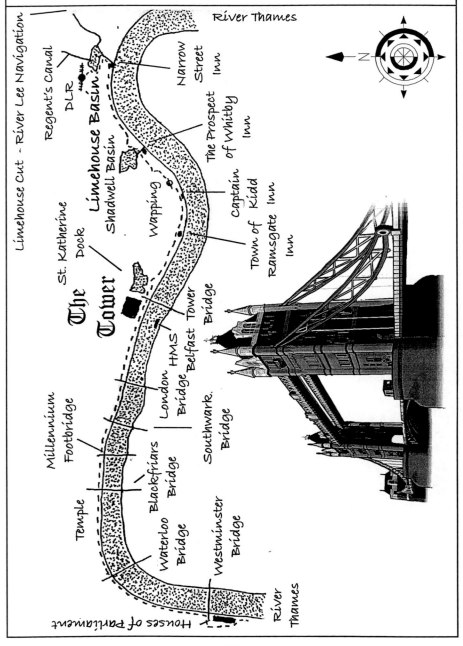

River Thames

N

Limehouse Cut - River Lee Navigation

Regent's Canal

DLR

Limehouse Basin

Shadwell Basin

St. Katherine Dock

Wapping

Narrow Street Inn

The Prospect of Whitby Inn

Captain of Kidd Inn

Town of Ramsgate Inn

The Tower

Tower Bridge

Belfast

HMS

London Bridge

Southwark Bridge

Millennium Footbridge

Temple

Blackfriars Bridge

Waterloo Bridge

Westminster Bridge

Houses of Parliament

River Thames

River Thames

RIVER THAMES - WESTMINSTER TO LIMEHOUSE BASIN
- 6 MILES
- allow 3 hours.

Basic route - Houses of Parliament - Westminster Bridge - Thames Path - Embankment - Waterloo Bridge - Temple - Blackfriars Bridge - Millennium Footbridge - Southwark Bridge - London Bridge - Custom House - The Tower - Tower Bridge - Wapping High Street - Shadwell Basin - Narrow Street - Limehouse Basin.

Map - O.S. 1:25,000 Explorer Series No. 173 - London North.

Start - Westminster Underground Station - District/Circle Line.
End - Limehouse Station - Docklands Light Railway.

Inns - Numerous along the way. In the latter stages - from Wapping onwards are several historical inns - Town of Ramsgate Inn. Captain Kidd Inn. The Prospect of Whitby Inn and Narrow Street Inn (Limehouse).

Teas - Several along the way especially in the Tower area - Tower Cafe.

ABOUT THE WALK - The final section from Westminster to Limehouse Basin, completing the 51 mile canal and river circuit - Limehouse Basin, Regent's Canal. Paddington Branch of the Grand Union Canal, Grand Union Canal to River Thames and River Thames from Richmond to Limehouse Basin. A magnificent two or three day walk! This section makes a very enjoyable walk in its own right, with so much to see on the way - the bridges and The Tower. The final two miles from The Tower via Wapping is a peaceful route past basins and old wharves.

WALKING INSTRUCTIONS - Exit the station - or continue your walk - and turn left, along Bridge Street, past the northern end of the Houses of

Parliament and Big Ben to **Westminster** Bridge. Turn left before it, **along Victoria** Embankment, on the signed Thames Path. The next couple of miles are pavement walking. Pass **Embankment** station, then Cleopatra's **Needle** and the Queen Mary before **Waterloo** Bridge. Then on past Somerset House and Temple Station. Pass the **boats**, HQS Wellington and HMS **President** and Unilever House on the left **before** passing under Blackfriars **Bridge. Continue** by the Thames and pass **under the** Millennium Footbridge - from St. **Paul's** to the Tate Modern Galley **on the** South Bank. Walk along Paul's **Walk and Three** Barrels Walk past The Ba**nker Inn** before reaching Southwark **Bridge. Ascend** steps to the road and cross **over** and descend steps to continue **by the river** along Three Grapes Walk **and W**aterman's Walk to London **Bridge. Continue** on the path with The M**onument** on the left and Custom House. **Soon after** is HMS Belfast (WW I I **Cruiser**) on the other side of the river. **Continue past** the Tower entrance by the **river**, past Traitor's Gate to Tower **Bridge.**

HMS Belfast.

Keep ahead passing a monument to a Dolphin and Girl with St. **Katherine's** Docks on the left. Soon after **you** leave the Thames as you walk **along Wapping** High Street, passing several **inns** - Town of Ramsgate Inn, where **Judge Jeffries** was caught and taken to The **Tower**, where he died one year later. **The past** Captain Kidd Inn and Wap**ping** Station; here a path sign sign states, **Limehouse** Basin I 1/4 miles. Soon **after follow** the road left then turn right **to pass The** Prospect of Whitby Inn an**d Shad**well Basin on the left. Just after **turn right to** follow streets past Wharves **to** Narrow Street and its inn. Just **after cross the** entrance to Limehouse Basi**n and** turn left and left again over **the lock gates.** Walk past the lock keeper**s hex**agonal building and continue **around the** lefthand side of the basin; **to your** right you can see the Lime**house Cut and** start of the Regent's Canal, **where** the walks in this book began. **Turn left to** Limehouse DLR station.

Tower Bridge.

View to Canary Wharf, from near Limehouse Basin.

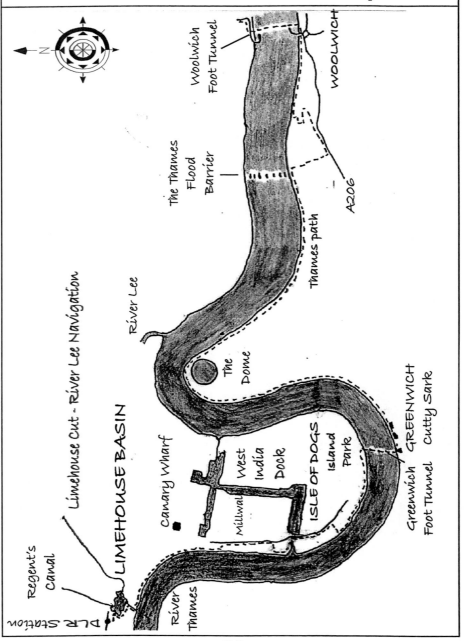

N

Regent's Canal

DLR Station

LIMEHOUSE BASIN

Limehouse Cut - River Lee Navigation

River Lee

River Thames

Canary Wharf

Millwal

West India Dock

ISLE OF DOGS

Island Park

The Dome

Thames path

The Thames Flood Barrier

Woolwich Foot Tunnel

WOOLWICH

A206

Greenwich Foot Tunnel

GREENWICH Cutty Sark

ISLE OF DOGS, RIVER THAMES, WOOLWICH, GREENWAY AND LIMEHOUSE CUT
- 20 MILES
- allow 8 hours.

Basic route - Limehouse Station - Limehouse Basin - River Thames Path - Millwall - Island Park - Greenwich Foot Tunnel - Greenwich - Thames Path - Millennium Dome - Greenwich Peninsula Ecology Park - The Thames Flood Barrier - Woolwich Ferry - Woolwich Foot Tunnel - King George V Dock - Royal Albert Dock - Capital Ring - Beckton Park - A13 - Greenway - Channelsea House - Three Mills Path - Three Mills Tide Mill - Bow Locks - Limehouse Cut - Limehouse Basin - Limehouse Station.

Map - O.S. 1:25,000 Explorer Series No. 162 - Greenwich and Gravesend.

Start and end - Limehouse Station, Docklands Light Railway.

Inns - Narrow Street - The Grapes, Booty's. City Pride Inn, just off the route near Canary Wharf. Ferry House Inn, near Greenwich foot tunnel - the oldest inn on the Isle of Dogs, c1722. Numerous in Greenwich, including just beyond on the path - Trafalgar Tavern, The Yacht Inn, and Cutty Sark Inn. Anchor & Hope Inn, near Thames Barrier. White Horse Inn on the A206. The Mitre Inn, Woolwich. Royal Standard Inn, North Woolwich.

Teas - Numerous in Greenwich. Terrace Cafe at the Thames Barrier Visitor's Centre. Three Mills.

ABOUT THE WALK - A long one but an exceptional walk on the eastern side of London. There is much to see on the way and the walk can be cut down into stages if necessary using the railway or Docklands Light Railway. Such as Greenwich - 6 miles. Woolwich - 11 miles. Cyprus DLR - 13 miles.

West Ham Underground Station - 17 miles.

First you walk round Limehouse Basin which you return to at the end. Then it is on along the Thames Path, past Canary Wharf and around Millwall to the Greenwich Foot Tunnel. Greenwich is well worth a look around with the Cutty Sark, Old Royal Naval College and Old Royal Observatory. Here the Greenwich Meridian and Time were initiated and are now so much a part of world life. Continuing on the Thames path you walk around the Greenwich Peninsula and Dome and onto the Thames Barrier. A final mile of the Thames brings you to Woolwich, where although there is a ferry, you should be a purest and walk through another foot tunnel, under the River Thames, to North Woolwich. Passing London City Airport, you follow the Capital Ring northwards around Beckton Park to the pedestrianised railway line - The Greenway. Following this for 2 1/2 miles, you leave it to gain the Tide Mills at Three Mills Island and the final section of the walk along the River Lee Navigation, along Limehouse Cut back to Limehouse Basin.

WALKING INSTRUCTIONS - From Limehouse Station, turn left and left again past a Garden Centre and cross the A101. Keep straight ahead into Limehouse Basin and walk around its righthand side to the hexagonal Lock Keepers House and turn right and left over the locks to Narrow Street. Turn left, now on the Thames Path and pass The Grapes Inn and Booty's. Just after turn right as Thames path signed, into Duke Shore Wharf (open 8.0. a.m. to 9.0 p.m. daily), to continue now beside the Thames. Pass the Royal China Restaurant and Canary Wharf Pier. Soon after cross a bridge with the City Pride Inn to your left. Continue beside the Thames for another 1/2 mile to a park, Arnhem Wharf and Millwall - named after a row of seven windmills to grind corn here. Turn left to the A1206 road and right to pass the Docklands Sailing Club and Millwall Lock - *Once the largest lock in London, giving access from the River Thames of Millwall Dock. Measured 80 ft (24m.) wide by 250 feet (76m.) long. Six hydraulic lock gates secured the lock, which as built in 1868. Badly bombed in 1940 and was never used again.*

At Devonshire House, No. 216, West Ferry Road return to the Thames at Maritime Quay. Soon reach the launch site of Isambard Kingdom Brunel's boat, *The Great Eastern. Launched on January 31st. 1858, at the fourteenth attempt, the boat cost £920,000 to build by 2,000 people. There was room for 800 First Class Passengers and 3,000 Second Class or 10,000 troops. Although well ahead of its day, it was not financially viable - carrying 12,000 tons of coal it travelled at 14 knots - and after sixteen years was used in an exhibition before being broken up.*

88

Launch site of The Great Eastern.

Continue beside the Thames to the Elephant Royal (Thai restaurant). Turn left to Ferry Street and the Ferry House Inn. Continue along Ferry Street to Island Park and the circular domed entrance to the Greenwich foot tunnel. Descend steps or take the life and walk through the tunnel, built in 1902, to Greenwich. *The tunnel cost £127,000 and is 1,277 feet long and 33 feet below the River Thames; 200,000 white tiles line the walkway.* Ahead is the Cutty Sark and Greenwich town to explore.

Greenwich Foot Tunnel Plaque.

The Cutty Sark, Greenwich.
- *the fastest tea clipper ever built, with masts and* 11 **miles** *of rigging.*

The Old Royal Naval College, Greenwich.

Turn left to continue along the Thames path past the Old Royal Naval College. Pass the Trafalgar Tavern and The Yacht Inn before The Trinity Hospital, dated 1614. Since 1617 this has been the home to 21 retired Gentlemen of Greenwich. Continue past a large iron anchor with a history plaque and the Cutty Sark Inn. A path signpost here states the Thames Barrier is 2 3/4 miles and Tower Bridge 5 1/2 miles! Continue beside the Thames past wharves and Tate & Lyle factory, always following the path signs for the Dome, and keeping the river on your left. In more than a mile from the Cutty Sark Inn at Ordnance Jetty reach the Greenwich Meridian marker with the path signs - Thames Barrier 2 miles and Waterloo Station 9 1/2 miles. Now with the Dome on your right follow the wide path around waters edge to the Dome's Jetty and sculpture - Quantum Cloud by Antony Gormley. Continue by the river and more than 1/2 mile later reach the Greenwich Peninsula Ecology Parkland and Greenwich Yacht Club. On the river is Bugsby's Reach and near here was Bugsby Hole. Here in the 18th. century people were gibbeted for three tides and assumed dead!

Quantum Cloud by Anthony Gormey.

Waterloo Station 8 1/2 miles; Thames Barrier 2 miles and poem on the base by David Dudgeon, 1999.

View back to The Dome and Canary Wharf.

Continue now on a road near the river with oyster catchers on the shore and the Thames Barrier ahead. Pass the Anchor & Hope Inn and reach the Thames Flood Barrier, with a Visitor's Centre and Terrace Cafe. Walk under the barrier and the side wall shows the whole of the River Thames from its source to the sea - see many places you have walked past! Just after and before the cafe, turn right and follow Cycle path No. 1, through gardens to the former Thames Barrier Arms - now a vet's surgery. Continue straight ahead to the A206 road. Turn left and pass the White Horse Inn and onto a roundabout. Take the second road on your left - Rushton Road - and follow the Thames Path signs upon reaching houses as you walk left, right and left again to reach the Thames. Keep beside it for 3/4 mile, over a footbridge and past two cannons to the Woolwich Ferry Road. Go straight across - unless taking the ferry - and descend to the Woolwich Foot Tunnel - built October 1912 and cost £87,000. Descend in the lift and walk 1,655 feet under the Thames to the other life and ascend to North Woolwich.

WOOLWICH TO LIMEHOUSE BASIN
- 9 MILES - *Map Two.*

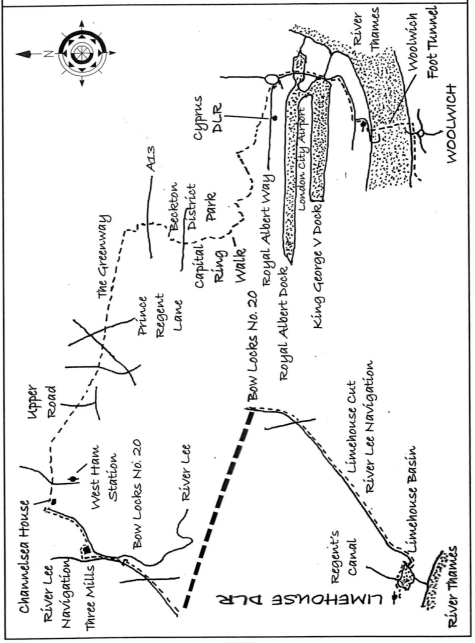

The Thames Barrier - Built in 1982 and until 2030, is expected to protect London from flooding. The gates take 30 minutes to close and are 15 metres high.

Turn right along the road, past the Old Station (Museum) to the Royal Standard Inn. Turn right along Albert Road (A112). You are now following the Capital Ring for the next five miles - it is all well signed. Cross Sir Steve Redgrave Bridge over the entrance to King George V Dock with the London City Airport in the middle and the Royal Albert Dock beyond. Reaching a large roundabout, cross two roads on your left; the latter being the Royal Albert Way and turn left onto the "path" of the Capital Ring. Keep ahead soon along The Ferndale with Cyprus DLR Station on your left. Just after pass houses with the sign - Beckton District Park, 1 mile. Pass Learoyd Gardens and gain New Beckton Park. Keep around its edge, first right then left to near a road and path sign - Greenway (Plaistow) 2 miles - part of your route. Follow the path around the righthand side of Beckton District Park to a road. Go straight across and continue in the park, along its righthand side with a lake well to your left, and reach the A13 road. Cross via a large footbridge and walk along Noel Road. Turn left along Roman Road and right along Stokes road to steps giving access to The Greenway.

Turn left and keep on this pedestrianised former railway line for the next 2 1/2 miles (50 mins.). In 3/4 mile cross your first road- Prince Regent Lane and onto three more in the 3/4 mile, the last one being Upper Road. More than 1/4 mile later cross a bridge over a railway line and 1/4 mile later the path on your left down steps to West Ham Stations. Continue a little further to Channelsea House on your left. Immediately after turn left, as path sign - Three Mills - leaving the Capital Ring. Keep the tidal river on your left all the way, crossing a bridge part over another river on your right. Continue by the river on the left to Three Mills. Reaching the cobbled courtyard, turn left past the mills to the bridge over the River Lee Navigation. But before it turn left to walk along the towpath. In 1/4 mile walk over the white bridge over Bow Locks No. 20 and continue now along the Limehouse Cut and follow it for 1 1/2 mile back to Limehouse Basin.

Reaching the basin turn right over the first footbridge and walk around the basin in an anti-clock wise direction. Pass houses on the left before the start of the Regent's Canal on the right via a footbridge, and keep ahead to your start out path and cross the road back to the Garden Centre and onto Limehouse Station.

Clock House Mill, Three Mills Island.

Bow Locks and Canary Wharf beyond.

RIVER LEE NAVIGATION -

*Length - Limehouse Basin, Bow to Hertford - 27 3/4 miles.
19 locks.*

The River Lee has been, since Roman times, an important trade route to London. An Act of 1571 for an artificial cut was made to help speed up the traffic. At the same time a pound at Waltham Abbey with lock gates - a similar principal to today - was made and is one of the earliest in the country. During the 18th and 19th. century the navigation was improved, these included in 1769 the Waltham, Edmonton and Hackney Cuts (avoiding the River Lee) and pound locks was opened. In 1911 The Lee Conservancy bought the River Stort Navigation and improved it together with the River Lee. By 1930, 130 ton boats could reach Enfield and 100 ton to Ware and Hertford. During the rest of the 20th. century many improvements were made including mechanised locks. Whilst many of the locks vary in size the majority are - 85 ft long by 16 ft wide and between 5 and 7 feet deep. Upto Enfield Lock they are double locks and beyond to Hertford, single locks. The river can be either spelt Lee or Lea.

U.K. CANAL MUSEUMS -

The London Canal Museum,
12-13, New Wharf Road,
London
N1 9RT
Tel: 020 7713 0836

National Waterways Museum,
Llanthony Warehouse,
Gloucester Docks,
Gloucester,
GL1 2EH
Tel: 01452 318054

The Canal Museum,
Stoke Bruerne,
Towcester,
Northamptonshire
NN12 7SE
Tel: 01604 862229

Foxton Canal Museum,
Middle Lock,
Gumley Road,
Foxton,
Market Harbourough,
Leicestershire
LE17 7RT
Tel: 0116 2792 657

The Boat Museum,
Ellesmere Port,
Cheshire
L65 4FW
Tel: 0151 355 5017

Union Canal Museum,
Manse Road,
Canal Basin,
Linlithgow,
West Lothian,
Scotland
Tel: 01506 671215

The Waterways Museum,
Dutch River Side,
Goole,
East Yorkshire
DN14 5TB
Tel: 01405 768730

Kennet and Avon Canal Museum,
Devizes Wharf,
Couch Lane,
Devizes,
Wiltshire
SN10 1EB
Tel: 01380 729489

Basingstoke Canal Centre,
Mytchett Place Road,
Mytchett,
Surrey
GU16 6DD
Tel: 01252 370073

WALK RECORD CHART

Regent's Canal -

Regent's Canal - Limehouse basin to Islington Tunnel - 4 miles ....

Mini Canal Ring - Regent's, Hertford Union & River Lee

Navigation - 6 miles ....

Islington to Little Venice - 4 1/2 miles ....

Little Venice to Islington, via River Thames - 8 miles ....

Grand Union Canal -

The Grand Union Canal - Paddington Branch - Little Venice

to Alperton - 6 1/2 miles ....

Alperton, Grand Union Canal and Brent River - 17 miles ....

Grand Union Canal, Hanwell Flight, Osterley Park,

Syon House and River Thames - 12 miles...

The River Thames

River Thames - Richmond to Westminster - 18 miles ....

River Thames - Westminster to Limehouse Basin - 6 miles ....

Isle of Dogs, River Thames, Woolwich, Greenway and

the Limehouse Cut - 20 miles ....

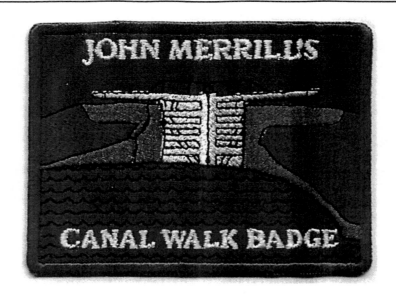

THE JOHN MERRILL CANAL WALK BADGE

Complete six walks in this book and get the above special
embroidered badge and special signed certificate. Badges are Blue cloth
with lettering and lock embroidered in four colours.

██ BADGE ORDER FORM ██

Date walks completed...

NAME ....

ADDRESS ....

....

Price: £6.00 each including postage, packing, VAT and signed completion
certificate. Amount enclosed (Payable to The John Merrill Foundation) ..
From: THE JOHN MERRILL FOUNDATION,
32, Holmesdale, Waltham Cross, Hertfordshire EN8 8QY
HAPPY WALKING T SHIRT - white & 4 colours - £10.00
e-mail - marathonhiker@aol.com
www.johnmerrillwalkguides.co.uk

********** *YOU MAY PHOTOCOPY THIS FORM* ***********

100

OTHER CANAL WALK GUIDES
by John N. Merrill

VOL ONE - DERBYSHIRE AND NOTTINGHAMSHIRE - More than 30 walks, both short and long, on the Erewash, Derby, Trent & Mersey, Nottingham, Beeston and Nutbrook canals. The guide is not just a walk guide but a historical guide to what can be seen today and a photographic essay to canals in the area. 128 pages 60 photographs 32 maps
ISBN 1-903627-53 -2 £10.95 - wire bound new enlarged edition

VOL TWO - CHESHIRE AND STAFFORDSHIRE - Details more than 40 circular walks on the Peak Forest, Macclesfield Caldon and Trent & Mersey canals. Like Vol. 1, a major reference source to canal walking on the western side of the Pennines. All are circular and include both long and short walks with numerous pubs along the way. 88 pages 61 photographs 27 maps ISBN 0 907496 38 5 Wire bound. £8.95

VOL THREE—STAFFORDSHIRE - 36 short circular walks on the Trent & Mersey, Coventry, Staffordshire & Worcestershire Canals within the boundary of Staffordshire, between Stoke on Trent and Burton Upon Trent. This book links together Vol. 1 & 2 of the series. 84 pages 60 photographs 30 maps ISBN 0 907496 62 8 Wire bound £8.95

VOL FOUR—THE CHESHIRE RING - Walk guide with history notes to the 97 mile walk around the ring on the Macclesfield, Peak Forest, Ashton, Rochdale, Bridgewater, and Trent & Mersey Canals. Comprehensive amenities guide to enable you to walk it in stages or as a weeks walk. 80 pages 38 photographs 15 maps ISBN 1-903627-39-7 £8.95 wire bound.
New edition

VOL FIVE—THE GRANTHAM CANAL More than fifteen walks on the Grantham Canal, from the River Trent to Grantham. Unspoilt walking in the Vale of Belvoir. 96 pages 45 photographs 16 maps
ISBN 1-903627-56-7 £9.95 NEW

WALKING THE TRENT & MERSEY CANAL - Walk guide to the whole length of the canal—end-to-end—from Preston Brook to Shardlow and Derwent Mouth. 93 miles of some of the finest canal walking in Britain. Amenities guide and walk described in stages. 64 pages 35 photographs 18 maps ISBN 1 874754 19 5.   £6.95

WALKING THE LLANGOLLEN CANAL A complete end to end walk from Nantwich to Llangollen -50 miles, along the canl. The scenery is oustanding and the canal features are unsurpassed. ISBN 1 84173 017 3 56 pages. 25 photographs. 10 maps. £5.95

WALKING THE DERBY CANAL RING - A magnificent 28 mile walk from the centre of Derby, following the line of the Derby Canal to the Trent & Mersey Canal and onto the River Trent and Erewash Canal. You return to Derby along the line of the Sandiacre section of the Derby Canal. ISBN 1874754 28 4. 32 pages. 5 maps. 10 photographs. £4.95

THE SALT & SAILS TRAIL by David Burkhill Howarth. - A magnificent 20 mile walk from Weston Point to Winsford along the Weaver Navigation in Cheshire, with very detailed history notes. ISBN 1 874754 58 6. 44 pages. 7 maps. 10 photographs. £5.95

SHORT CIRCULAR WALKS IN THE CHESTERFIELD CANAL More than fifteen walks on the Chesterfield Canall, from Chesterfield via Worksop to the River Trent at West Stockwith. Unspoilt walking Derbyshire & Nottinghamshire. 112 pages 45 photographs 16 maps ISBN 1-903627-56-7 £10.95. Colour edition £14.95. Wire bound.

SHORT CIRCULAR WALKS ON THE CROMFORD CANAL Ten walks on the Cromford Canal, from Cromford to the Great Northern Basin at Langley.. Unspoilt walking, tracing the abandoned canal and Pinxton Arm. 96 pages 45 photographs 16 maps ISBN 1-903627-54-0 £8.95. Colour edition £10.95 Wire bound.

SHORT CIRCULAR WALKS ON THE RIVER LEE NAVIGATION - (London to Hertford) - Northern Volume.
60 pages, 23 photographs, 10 detailed maps and walks - walks between Ponders End Lock and Hertford. History notes. ISBN 1-903627-68-0 £7.95 **NEW**

SHORT CIRCULAR WALKS ON THE RIVER STORT NAVIGATION
Despite only being 13 1/2 miles long from the River Lee Navigation, near Broxbourne to Bishop's Stortford, the navigation is a gem and full of history. Eight circular walks explore its full length and one explores it end to end. The guide is not just a walk one, but a history of the canal and surrounding villages and a photographic essay.
92 pages, 68 colour photographs, 12 maps. Wire bound.
ISBN 1-903627-73-7 £10.95 **NEW**

SHORT CIRCULAR WALKS ON THE RIVER LEE NAVIGATION - (London to Hertford) - Southern Volume.
68 pages, 33 photographs, 12 detailed maps and walks - walks between Limehouse Basin/River Thames and Enfield Lock. Includes Bow Creek River and City Mill Rivers. Includes 28 mile end to end walk - Limehouse Basin to Hertford.
Considerable History notes. ISBN 1-903627-74-5 £7.95 **NEW**

WALKING THE CANALS OF LONDON
End to End walks and circular walks on the Regent's Canal and Union Canal and the Paddington Branch, and exploraton of the Isle of Dogs and River Thames. Plus a London Canal Loop walk of 52 miles.
104 pages. 96 colour photographs. 18 maps. Wire Bound.
ISBN 978-0-9553691-2-4 £10.95 **NEW**

WALKING THE RIVER LEE NAVIGATION - 20 walks.
Both the South and North volumes in one book, plus additional walks around the 2012 Olympic Park area. ISBN 978-09553691-8-6 108 pages. Wire bound. £9.95 NEW

SHORT CIRCULAR WALKS IN THE COLNE VALLEY (Grand Union Canal) 8 walks - 3 to 11 miles long - that full eplore the area between Rickmansworth and Slough. One 20 mile walk - Rickmansworth to the River Thames.
72 pages. 12 maps. 40 photographs. ISBN 978-0-9560649-5-0 £7.95 NEW

WALKING THE CHELMER AND BLACKWATER NAVIGATION - 16 MILES - From Maldon to Chelmsford, Essex, beside this stunning and unspoilt waterway. NEW 2011

OTHER BOOKS by Revd. John N. Merrill

CIRCULAR WALK GUIDES -

SHORT CIRCULAR WALKS IN THE PEAK DISTRICT - Vols. 1 to 9
CIRCULAR WALKS IN WESTERN PEAKLAND
SHORT CIRCULAR WALKS IN THE STAFFORDSHIRE MOORLANDS
SHORT CIRCULAR WALKS - TOWNS & VILLAGES OF THE PEAK DISTRICT
SHORT CIRCULAR WALKS AROUND MATLOCK
SHORT CIRCULAR WALKS IN "PEAK PRACTICE COUNTRY."
SHORT CIRCULAR WALKS IN THE DUKERIES
SHORT CIRCULAR WALKS IN SOUTH YORKSHIRE
SHORT CIRCULAR WALKS IN SOUTH DERBYSHIRE
SHORT CIRCULAR WALKS AROUND BUXTON
SHORT CIRCULAR WALKS AROUND WIRKSWORTH
SHORT CIRCULAR WALKS IN THE HOPE VALLEY
40 SHORT CIRCULAR WALKS IN THE PEAK DISTRICT
CIRCULAR WALKS ON KINDER & BLEAKLOW
SHORT CIRCULAR WALKS IN SOUTH NOTTINGHAMSHIRE
SHORT CIRCULAR WALKS IN CHESHIRE
SHORT CIRCULAR WALKS IN WEST YORKSHIRE
WHITE PEAK DISTRICT AIRCRAFT WRECKS
CIRCULAR WALKS IN THE DERBYSHIRE DALES
SHORT CIRCULAR WALKS FROM BAKEWELL
SHORT CIRCULAR WALKS IN LATHKILL DALE
CIRCULAR WALKS IN THE WHITE PEAK
SHORT CIRCULAR WALKS IN EAST DEVON
SHORT CIRCULAR WALKS AROUND HARROGATE
SHORT CIRCULAR WALKS IN CHARNWOOD FOREST
SHORT CIRCULAR WALKS AROUND CHESTERFIELD
SHORT CIRCULAR WALKS IN THE YORKS DALES - Vol 1 - Southern area.
SHORT CIRCULAR WALKS IN THE AMBER VALLEY (Derbyshire)
SHORT CIRCULAR WALKS IN THE LAKE DISTRICT
SHORT CIRCULAR WALKS IN THE NORTH YORKSHIRE MOORS
SHORT CIRCULAR WALKS IN EAST STAFFORDSHIRE
LONG CIRCULAR WALKS IN THE PEAK DISTRICT - Vol.1 to 5.
DARK PEAK AIRCRAFT WRECK WALKS
LONG CIRCULAR WALKS IN THE STAFFORDSHIRE MOORLANDS
LONG CIRCULAR WALKS IN CHESHIRE
WALKING THE TISSINGTON TRAIL
WALKING THE HIGH PEAK TRAIL
WALKING THE MONSAL TRAIL & SETT VALLEY TRAILS
PEAK DISTRICT WALKING - TEN "TEN MILER'S" - Vol 1 and 2.
CLIMB THE PEAKS OF THE PEAK DISTRICT
PEAK DISTRICT WALK A MONTH Vols One,Two, Three, Four, Five & Six
TRAIN TO WALK Vol. One - The Hope Valley Line
DERBYSHIRE LOST VILLAGE WALKS -Vol One and Two.
CIRCULAR WALKS IN DOVEDALE AND THE MANIFOLD VALLEY
CIRCULAR WALKS AROUND GLOSSOP
WALKING THE LONGDENDALE TRAIL
WALKING THE UPPER DON TRAIL
SHORT CIRCULAR WALKS IN CANNOCK CHASE
CIRCULAR WALKS IN THE DERWENT VALLEY
WALKING THE TRAILS OF NORTH-EAST DERBYSHIRE
WALKING THE PENNINE BRIDLEWAY & CIRCULAR WALKS
SHORT CIRCULAR WALKS ON THE NEW RIVER & SOUTH-EAST HERTFORDSHIRE
SHORT CIRCULAR WALKS IN EPPING FOREST
SHORT CIRCULAR WALKS AROUND SAFFRON WALDEN

WALKING THE STREETS OF LONDON
LONG CIRCULAR WALKS IN EASTERN HERTFORDSHIRE
LONG CIRCULAR WALKS IN WESTERN HERTFORDSHIRE
WALKS IN THE LONDON BOROUGH OF ENFIELD
WALKS IN THE LONDON BOROUGH OF BARNET
WALKS IN THE LONDON BOROUGH OF HARINGEY
WALK IN THE LONDON BOROUGH OF WALTHAM FOREST
SHORT CIRCULAR WALKS AROUND HERTFORD
THE BIG WALKS OF LONDON
SHORT CIRCULAR WALKS AROUND BISHOP'S STORTFORD
SHORT CIRCULAR WALKS AROUND EPPING DISTRICT
CIRCULAR WALKS IN THE BOROUGH OF BROXBOURNE
LONDON INTERFAITH WALKS - Vol 1 and Vol. 2
LONG CIRCULAR WALKS IN THE NORTH CHILTERNS
SHORT CIRCULAR WALKS IN EASTERN HERTFORDSHIRE
WORCESTERSHIRE VILLAGE WALKS by Des Wright
WARWICKSHIRE VILLAGE WALKS by Des Wright
WALKING AROUND THE ROYAL PARKS OF LONDON
WALKS IN THE LONDON BOROUGH OF CHELSEA AND ROYAL KENSINGTON

CANAL WALKS -

VOL 1 - DERBYSHIRE & NOTTINGHAMSHIRE
VOL 2 - CHESHIRE & STAFFORDSHIRE
VOL 3 - STAFFORDSHIRE
VOL 4 - THE CHESHIRE RING
VOL 5 - THE GRANTHAM CANAL
VOL 6 - SOUTH YORKSHIRE
VOL 7 - THE TRENT & MERSEY CANAL
VOL 8 - WALKING THE DERBY CANAL RING
VOL 9 - WALKING THE LLANGOLLEN CANAL
VOL 10 - CIRCULAR WALKS ON THE CHESTERFIELD CANAL
VOL 11 - CIRCULAR WALKS ON THE CROMFORD CANAL
Vol.13 - SHORT CIRCULAR WALKS ON THE RIVER LEE NAVIGATION -Vol. 1 - North
Vol. 14 - SHORT CIRCULAR WALKS ON THE RIVER STORT NAVIGATION
Vol.15 - SHORT CIRCULAR WALKS ON THE RIVER LEE NAVIGATION - Vol. 2 - South
Vol. 16 - WALKING THE CANALS OF LONDON
Vol 17 - WALKING THE RIVER LEE NAVIGATION
Vol. 20 - SHORT CIRCULAR WALKS IN THE COLNE VALLEY
Vol 21 - THE BLACKWATER & CHELMER NAVIGATION - End to End.
Vol. 22 - NOTTINGHAM'S LOST CANAL by Bernard Chell.
Vol. 23 - WALKING THE RIVER WEY & GODALMING NAVIAGTIONS END TO END
Vol.25 - WALKING THE GRAND UNION CANAL - LONDON TO BIRMINGHAM.

JOHN MERRILL DAY CHALLENGE WALKS

WHITE PEAK CHALLENGE WALK
THE HAPPY HIKER - WHITE PEAK - CHALLENGE WALK
DARK PEAK CHALLENGE WALK
PEAK DISTRICT END TO END WALKS
STAFFORDSHIRE MOORLANDS CHALLENGE WALK

JOHN MERRILL DAY CHALLENGE WALKS

WHITE PEAK CHALLENGE WALK
THE HAPPY HIKER - WHITE PEAK - CHALLENGE WALK No.2
DARK PEAK CHALLENGE WALK
PEAK DISTRICT END TO END WALKS
STAFFORDSHIRE MOORLANDS CHALLENGE WALK
THE LITTLE JOHN CHALLENGE WALK
YORKSHIRE DALES CHALLENGE WALK
NORTH YORKSHIRE MOORS CHALLENGE WALK
LAKELAND CHALLENGE WALK
THE RUTLAND WATER CHALLENGE WALK
MALVERN HILLS CHALLENGE WALK
THE SALTERIS WAY
THE SNOWDON CHALLENGE
CHARNWOOD FOREST CHALLENGE WALK
THREE COUNTIES CHALLENGE WALK (Peak District).
CAL-DER-WENT WALK
THE QUANTOCK WAY
BELVOIR WITCHES CHALLENGE WALK
THE CARNEDDAU CHALLENGE WALK
THE SWEET PEA CHALLENGE WALK
THE LINCOLNSHIRE WOLDS - BLACK DEATH - CHALLENGE WALK
JENNIFER'S CHALLENGE WALK
THE EPPING FOREST CHALLENGE WALK
THE THREE BOROUGH CHALLENGE WALK - NORTH LONDON
THE HERTFORD CHALLENGE WALK
THE BOSHAM CHALLENGE WALK
THE KING JOHN CHALLENGE WALK
THE NORFOLK BROADS CHALLENGE WALK
THE RIVER MIMRAM WALK
THE ISLE OF THANET CHHALENGE WALK
EAST DEVON CHALLENGE WALK

INSTRUCTION & RECORD -

HIKE TO BE FIT.....STROLLING WITH JOHN
THE JOHN MERRILL WALK RECORD BOOK
HIKE THE WORLD - John Merrill's guide to walking & Backpacking.

MULTIPLE DAY WALKS -

THE RIVERS'S WAY
PEAK DISTRICT: HIGH LEVEL ROUTE
PEAK DISTRICT MARATHONS
THE LIMEY WAY
THE PEAKLAND WAY
COMPO'S WAY by Alan Hiley
THE BRIGHTON WAY

COAST WALKS & NATIONAL TRAILS -

ISLE OF WIGHT COAST PATH
PEMBROKESHIRE COAST PATH
THE CLEVELAND WAY
WALKING ANGELSEY'S COASTLINE.
WALKING THE COASTLINE OF THE CHANNEL ISLANDS
THE ISLE OF MAN COASTAL PATH - "The Way of the Gull."
A WALK AROUND HAYLING ISLAND
A WALK AROUND THE ISLE OF SHEPPEY
A WALK AROUND THE ISLE OF JERSEY
WALKING AROUND THE ISLANDS OF ESSEX

DERBYSHIRE & PEAK DISTRICT HISTORICAL GUIDES -

A to Z GUIDE OF THE PEAK DISTRICT
DERBYSHIRE INNS - an A to Z guide
HALLS AND CASTLES OF THE PEAK DISTRICT & DERBYSHIRE
TOURING THE PEAK DISTRICT & DERBYSHIRE BY CAR
DERBYSHIRE FOLKLORE
PUNISHMENT IN DERBYSHIRE
CUSTOMS OF THE PEAK DISTRICT & DERBYSHIRE
WINSTER - a souvenir guide
ARKWRIGHT OF CROMFORD
LEGENDS OF DERBYSHIRE
DERBYSHIRE FACTS & RECORDS
TALES FROM THE MINES by Geoffrey Carr
PEAK DISTRICT PLACE NAMES by Martin Spray
DERBYSHIRE THROUGH THE AGES - Vol 1 -DERBYSHIRE IN PREHISTORIC TIMES
SIR JOSEPH PAXTON
FLORENCE NIGHTINGALE
JOHN SMEDLEY
BONNIE PRINCE CHARLIE & 20 mile walk.
THE STORY OF THE EARLS AND DUKES OF DEVONSHIRE

JOHN MERRILL'S MAJOR WALKS -

TURN RIGHT AT LAND'S END
WITH MUSTARD ON MY BACK
TURN RIGHT AT DEATH VALLEY
EMERALD COAST WALK
I CHOSE TO WALK - Why I walk etc.
A WALK IN OHIO - 1,310 miles around the Buckeye Trail.
I AM GUIDED - the story of John's wal;king life.

SKETCH BOOKS -

SKETCHES OF THE PEAK DISTRICT

COLOUR BOOK:-

THE PEAK DISTRICT.......something to remember her by.

OVERSEAS GUIDES -

HIKING IN NEW MEXICO - Vol I - The Sandia and Manzano Mountains.
Vol 2 - Hiking "Billy the Kid" Country.
Vol 4 - N.W. area - " Hiking Indian Country."
"WALKING IN DRACULA COUNTRY" - Romania.
WALKING THE TRAILS OF THE HONG KONG ISLANDS.

VISITOR GUIDES - MATLOCK . BAKEWELL.

ASHBOURNE.

See all my books on -
www.johnmerrillwalkguides.co.uk

Pilgrim Guides -
www.thejohnmerrillministry.co.uk

NEW LONDON WALK GUIDES

WALKING THE CANALS OF LONDON

Nine walks fully exploring - The Regents Canal, Grand Union Canal (Paddington Branch), River Thames and Isle of Dogs and the "London Canal Loop".
A5 wire bound. 108 pages. 13 maps. 95 b/w photographs.

£10.95   ISBN 978-0-9553691-2-4

WALKING THE STREETS OF LONDON

7 historical short walks - 2 to 6 miles long and allowing - 4 TO 5 HOURS - in the city with basic themes -

"The Great Fire', "Wigs & Pens".
The Good and Gracious".
"The Royal Palaces", "The Hot Spots",
"Bridges, Boats and Dungeons".
"Monks, murder, punishment and poetry".

A5 wire bound. 112 pages. 9 maps. 84 b/w photographs.

£10.95   ISBN 978-0-9553691-1-7

LONDON INTERFAITH WALKS - Vol. One & Two

Seven walks in London to all the major religious sites.
Themed walks - Christian, Buddhist, Hindu etc.
. A5 Wire bound. 112 pages. 10 maps   130 photos.
     £10.95
ISBN 978-0-9568044-3-3

See all our books on our website -
www.johnmerrillwalkguides.co.uk

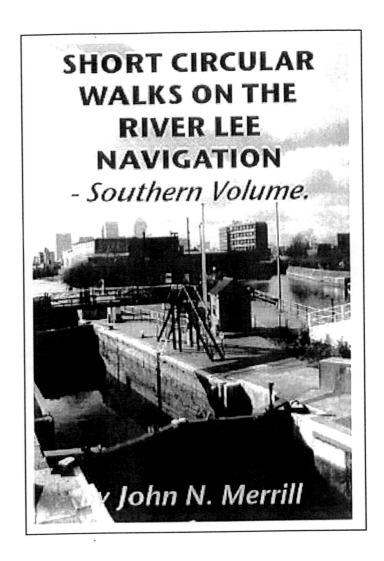

SHORT CIRCULAR WALKS ON THE RIVER LEE NAVIGATION
- Vol 2 - Southern Half.
- 5 walks between Limehouse Basin & Enfield Lock. Plus 28 mile End to End
Walk.
10 Maps. 38 b/w photos. 68 pages,
£6.95   NEW
ISBN 1-903627-74-5

OTHER NORTH LONDON WALK BOOKS
by JOHN N. MERRILL

SHORT CIRCULAR WALKS ON THE RIVER LEE NAVIGA-TION - Northern Volume -
Ponder's End - Hertford. 64 pages, 23 photographs, 10 detailed maps and walks. History notes.
- ISBN 1-903627-68-0 @ £8.50

WALKING THE RIVER LEE NAVIGATION - VOL 1 & 2.

SHORT CIRCULAR WALKS ON THE NEW RIVER & SOUTH EAST HERTFORDSHIRE
11 walks - 5 to 10 miles long between Waltham Cross and Hertford; many on the New River. New revised and enlarged edition 80 pages, 24 photographs, 13 detailed maps. History notes.
ISBN 1-903627-69-9 @ £8.95

SHORT CIRCULAR WALKS IN EPPING FOREST
10 circular walks 6 to 18 miles long. Combined they explore the whole forest and its surrounding area. 68 pages. 12 maps. 30 photographs. History notes.
ISBN 1-903627-72-9 @ £8.50

LONG CIRCULAR WALKS IN EASTERN HERTFORDSHIRE
9 walks - 15 to 20 miles long. Beautiful unspoilt walking in rolling countryside full of historical interest. £10.95
ISBN 978-0-9553691-7-9

LONG CIRCULAR WALKS IN WESTERN HERTFORDSHIRE -
9 long walks - 15 to 20 miles.. 112 pages. Wire bound. 55 photographs. 20 detailed maps. £10.95
ISBN 978-0-955651113

SHORT CIRCULAR WALKS AROUND HERTFORD.
3 historical Town walks and four country walks.
ISBN 978-0-9556511-7-5 £9.95

NEW - SHORT CIRCULAR WALKS AROUND BISHOP' STORTFORD

SHORT CIRCULAR WALKS ON THE RIVER STORT NAVIGATION
8 circular walks; 1 End to End walk. Full history and photographic study of this peaceful waterway. 92 pages. 68 photographgs. 12 maps. ISBN 1-903627- 73-7 £11.95

SHORT CIRCULAR WALKS ON THE RIVER LEE NAVIGATION - Southern Volume -
Limehouse basin to Hackney Marsh. 5 walks on the Regent Canal, Hertford Union and Limehouse Cut. Including Three Mills and its rivers. The guide also details a 28 mile End to End walk along the Navigation. 68 pages. 10 maps, 30 photographs.
ISBn 1-903627-74-5 £7.95

EPPING FOREST CHALLENGE WALK - 21 MILES.
Starts and ends at Waltham Abbey and takes in the whole forest. 44 pages. 6 maps. 10 photos £7.95
ISBN 978-0-9553691-0-0

"St. ALBANS WAY" - 26 mile Pilgrims walk from Waltham Abbey to St. Alban's Cathedral.
£7.95
ISBN 978-0-9553691-3-1

NORTH LONDON - THE THREE BOROUGH CHALLENGE WALK - 21 MILES
A walk linking together the three boroughs of Enfield, Barnet and Haringey.
A magnificent countryside walk. Certificate for the successful.
A5. 40 pages. Full colour book. ISBN 978-0-9556511-9-9
£7.95

NEW - SHORT CIRCULAR WALKS IN EPPING DISTRICT

Illustrated Talks
by Revd. John N. Merrill

John has countless talks on his recording breaking walks around the world.
For a full list contact John - Tel. 01992-762776
Email - marathonhiker@aol.com

His latest talks -

WALKING TO MONT ST. MICHEL - John has walked here twice - from Farnham via Winchester to Mont St. Michel (200 miles), and from Caen (100 miles) joining the annual pilgrimage walk organised by the Association of Chemins de Mont St. Michel. Both remarkable walks with the final 7km across the exposed sand, mud and rivers to the rock and abbey.

LONDON TO OXFORD PILGRIMAGE WALK - St. Frideswide Way - 93 miles. John discovers and traces the medieval pilgrimage route from Westminster Abbey to Christ Church Cathedral in Oxford, and the shrine of St. Frideswide. Then onto Binsey and her "forgotten" healing well; the Lourdes of the South.

WALKING ESSEX'S COASTLINE - 250 MILES - An exceptional walk around England's second largest county's coastline, rich in history, sea-birds and waders and more than 100 islands. A surprising journey.

WALKING MY WAY - The on going story of John's unique walking life, with some 219,000 miles walked. The stories and tales from his ground breaking walks around the world.

The London Canal Museum,
12-13, New Wharf Road,
London. N1 9RT.
Tel. 020 7713 0836
www.canalmuseum.org.uk

A WALK AROUND THE ISLE OF DOGS - 5 MILES

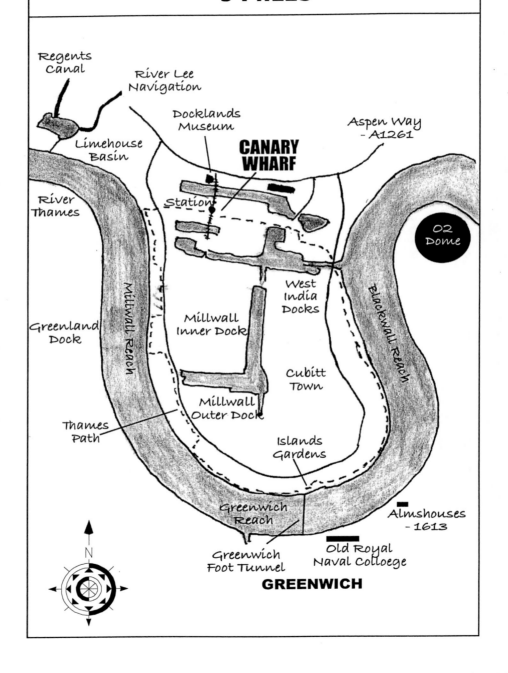

AROUND THE ISLE OF DOGS
- 5 MILES
- allow 2 to 3 hours.

Basic route - *Canary Wharf Station (DLR) - Thames Path - Millwall Reach - Millwall - Millwall Lock - West Ferry - Greenwich Reach - Island Gardens - Blackwall Reach - Pier Head Lock - South Dock - Canary Wharf.*

Map -*O.S. 1:25,000 Explorer Series No. 162 - Greenwich and Gravesend.*

Start and End - *Canary Wharf Station - Docklands Light Railway (DLR). Or West India Quay (DLR) station, near Docklands Museum.*

Inns - *City Pride Inn. The Ferry House Inn. Several in Canary Wharf.*

Cafe - *Island Gardens, beside Greenwich Foot Tunnel entrance. Several in Canary Wharf.*

ABOUT THE WALK - One of the gems of east London! A walk right around the island starting and ending amongst Britain's tallest buildings. You are also in the heart of Britain's financial district where suited city whiz kids rush by, as you walk comfortably in your boots, shorts and T shirt! The first half as you walk clockwise around the "island" is along the Thames Path to the Greenwich Foot Tunnel. Here in the Island Gardens you have fine views of Greenwich and the former Naval College. From here you continue beside the River Thames to the entrance to South Dock and walk back into Canary Wharf beneath the towering skyscrapers. If time permits a visit to the Docklands Museum - highly recommended - completes your education about this fascinating area. Every step brings you to countless historical features which makes the walk so enjoyable.

WALKING INSTRUCTIONS - Exit Canary Wharf Station and head west to Cabot Square. Keep straight ahead along West India Avenue to West Ferry

Road. Bear left and right and gain the well signed Thames Path, which you follow for the next two miles. Pass the City Pride Inn and reach the path above the shore of the River Thames. In 1/2 mile reach the site of seven windmills, which gave Millwall its name. Pass Arnhem Wharf and Sir John McDougal Gardens, before turning left away from the river to West Ferry Road. Turn right along the road past the Docklands Sailing Club (Millwall Outer Dock), on the left and Millwall Lock on the right. Continue on the road past St. Edmunds Roman Catholic church. Soon after at No 216 - Devonshire House, turn right and regain the embankment and Thames Path. Walk along Maritime Quay and pass the launch site of Brunel's boat - the Great Britain.

The Great Britain launch site.

Just after is the site of a Colour Works on the left. 1/4 mile later your turn left away from the river to reach the Ferry House Inn - the oldest on the island, c1722. Turn right along Ferry Street and reach Island Gardens and the entrance of the Greenwich Foot Tunnel. The cafe is on the left as you enter the gardens.

Greenwich Foot tunnel entrance, Island Gardens.

Walk to the river embankment for the views across the river to Greenwich, Royal Observatory and Old Royal Naval College. For the next 1 1/2 mile you basically walk along the embankment. First along Riverside Walk, then Cubitt Wharf and along Sauders Ness. Keeping close to the river walk along Dungeons Wharf and Millennium Wharf with views ahead to the 02 Dome. Pass the tragic monument to several fireman who were killed in an explosion. Soon after, when it is low tide you walk beside a real sandy beach, before walking along London Yard. Pass a tower block and Pier Head Lock, before passing the British Waterways Board Docklands Office on the right. Just after reach the main road, Preston's Road and bear right to cross the drawbridge over the entrance of the South Dock - West India Dock. Continue a few more strides before turning left, as path signed - Canary Wharf. The road passes near the docks on the left before turning right past the Docklands Communication area. Soon after with Blackwall Basin to your right, ascend steps to Churchill Place and the main buildings of Canary Wharf. Keep ahead beneath the towering buildings, along Churchill, Canada, and North Colonnade back to Canary Wharf Station. If you want to go to the Docklands Museum, continue ahead and turn right and cross a footbridge over a wharf and turn left to the museum in the wharf buildings; it is all well signed. From here you can return home from West India Quay (DLR) station, just to the right

In memory of those who
tragically lost their lives
following an explosion on this site,
(previously known as Dudgeons Wharf),
on the 17th July 1969

J. V. APPLEBY	London Fire Brigade
T. BREEN	,, ,, ,,
T. P. CARVOSSO	,, ,, ,,
M. W. GAMBLE	,, ,, ,,
A. C. SMEE	,, ,, ,,
R. ADAMS	A & R Metal Company

The 02 Dome from the Isle of Dogs.

Burrells Wharf.

Dock and Canary Wharf.

Docklands Museum -
Former Sugar warehouse built in 1802.
www.museumindocklands.org.uk

Walking the Grand Union Canal from London to Birmingham

The Hatton flight of locks.

by Revd. John N. Merrill

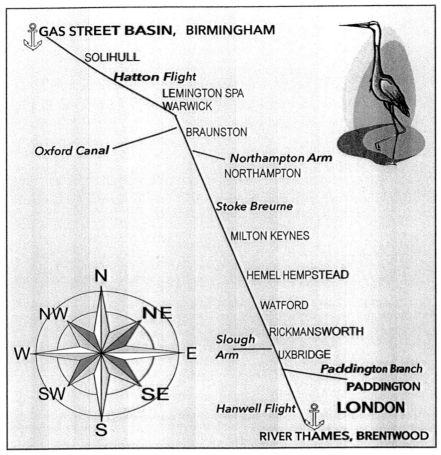

GAS STREET BASIN, BIRMINGHAM

SOLIHULL

Hatton Flight

LEMINGTON SPA
WARWICK

BRAUNSTON

Oxford Canal

Northampton Arm
NORTHAMPTON

Stoke Breurne

MILTON KEYNES

HEMEL HEMPSTEAD

WATFORD

RICKMANSWORTH

Slough Arm

UXBRIDGE

Paddington Branch
PADDINGTON

Hanwell Flight LONDON

RIVER THAMES, BRENTWOOD

N NW NE W E SW SE S

One of England's **finest** canal walks - 153 miles - **from the River Thames** to Gas **Street** Basin, Birmingham. Plus **the shorter** route along the Pad**dington** Branch. Can be done over **9 or more stages** with good inter**linking** transport at the end of **each stage**. Badge and certificate **for those** that complete the walk.

ISBN 978-099278766-0

9 780992 787660

£10.95

Canal Walks Series - Vol. 25.
"Hiking the sacred paths and trails of the world for others to follow."

THE JOHN MERRILL
FOUNDATION

Wherever you are, you are either

on or close to a

John Merrill Walk.

.........enjoy!

WALKING THE PURE WAY

I believe a walk, whatever the distance, should be done on two feet, with basics of life on your back and map/gps in your hand. When I first started the thought of missing a section and using transport was the death knoll to the walk. I could not live with myself if I had missed a section.

Today when I walk to Santiago de Compestella on a 1,000 mile route, I am saddened that many walkers take a bus here and there, missing out a section that was "boring". I could never understand, at first, having overtook a walker, a few days later they were ahead of me. They had certainly not passed me. When I walked the Pacific Crest Trail in America. I walked it all despite deep snow in the Sierra's. Many who get there because of snow and closed trails, bus round, missing 300 miles or more of trail. I had snow and had to walk beneath the mountains for four days before finding a way in. It still meant that I had full-filled my plan and walked from Mexico to Canada un-aided. And having reached Canada flew back to the High Sierra's and climbed them all. Then I went home feeling complete.'

Similarly on the Appalachian Trail, on reaching a Post Office where my food parcel was, I loaded my pack with 14 days of food and basics and headed back into the wilderness and emerged 14 days later at another Post Office and parcel. Today, few do it traditionally, opting to carry 3 days of food and hike & hitch-hike out to a food store. Makes no sense physically and mentally, and makes the walk twice as long.

Sadly today sport is tainted with performance enhancing drugs. I have never taken any drug, only half a dozen aspirins over the years, and never seen a doctor. To excel there is one simple method. Be totally devoted and singleminded at your sport and whilst getting to peak performance realise that it is not just physical but having the correct mindset to do it.

I walk for it is the most natural and life enhancing activity you can do. Plus there is never any age limit; you can still walk when you are a hundred. So walk naturally one foot in front of the other and enjoy the landscape and before you know it you are at your destination, regardless of the mileage and mountains on the way. Glow with pride at making it on your own feet all the way and in an untainted way.

Revd. John N. Merrill - May 2017.

WHY I WALK *by Revd. John N. Merrill*

I walk for the exercise; to stretch my legs and muscles; to suck in the fresh air and be free in the wide, wide world, as I walk upon Mother Earth.

I walk to see the trees; that sway in the breeze. To watch the leaves flutter in summer and to walk through on the ground in November. I observe the quietness of winter and watch the buds form ready to emerge when it is their time.

I walk to see the wild flowers; the wood anemones, the blue bells, red campion, and orchids that grow in Spring and early summer.

I walk to listen to the birds that sing in the hedgerows and trees. The friendly Robin is not far away, the started Jay or motionless heron standing at the waters edge. A sudden flash of blue as a kingfisher shoots by.

I walk to see the wild animals; the red fox, the deer, the squirrel and the insects and butterflies, like the dragonfly and red admiral butterfly.

I walk to see the views; to ascend a lofty peak and sit upon the summit surveying everything below, like an eagle high in the air.

I walk for solitude; peace and quiet, to go back to the basics of life, where it is just man and the elements.

I walk in the sunshine, the rain, snow and wind. All has its own beauty and characteristic. All are the cycles of life. I admire the cloudless sky and the rolling clouds of wind and storm.

I walk to see the work of man and God, knowing that we are all connected. Everything has its own beauty.

As the sun sets and I walk home, I know I have lived and experienced a full day, witnessing the whole spectrum of life. I am grateful, very grateful, that God gave me two fine legs, a healthy heart and good lungs to see paradise on Earth.

© Revd. John N. Merrill 2012

HOW TO DO A WALK

The walks in this book follow public right of ways, be it a footpath, bridleway, Boat or Rupp. which are marked on the Ordnance Survey 1:25,000 Explorer Series of maps.

On each walk I have detailed which map are needed and I would urge you to carry and use a map. As I walk I always have the map out on the section I am walking, constantly checking that I am walking the right way. Also when coming to any road or path junction, I can check on the map to ensure I take the right route.

Most paths are signed and waymarked with coloured arrows - yellow for footpaths; blue for bridleways - but I would at best describe them as intermittent. They act as confirmation of the right of way you are walking and the arrow usually point in the direction of travel.

The countryside has the added problem of vandalism and you will find path logo's and Information Boards spray painted over and even path signs pointing the wrong way! That is why I always advise carrying the map open on the area you are walking to check you are walking the right way. In my walking instructions I have given the name and number of each main and minor road, canal lock and bridge number, together with house numbers where you turn and the name of the inns passed. Wherever I add what the footpath sign says, plus the stiles, footbridges and kissing gates en route. All to help you have a smooth and trouble free walk.

I confirm that I have walked every route and written what I found at the time of walking.

Most people don't walk correctly with a straight spine and feet parallel to each other, and a few inches apart. Each step starts the cycle of lifting the foot a little way off the ground and placing the heel down first, then moving forward as the foot bends with the toes being last to leave the ground as the cycle begins again. It is all a gentle fluid rolling motion; with practice you can glide across the terrain, effortlessly, for mile after mile.

May the sun bring you new energy by day.
May the moon softly restore you by night.
May the rain wash away your worries.
May the breeze blow new strength into your being.
May you walk gbently through the world and
Know its beauty all the days of your life.

Apache blessing.

Look at the trees.
Look at the birds.
Look at the clouds.
Look at the stars ……..
And if you have eyes
you will be able to see
that the whole of
existence is joyful.

Osho.

THE JOHN MERRILL MINISTRY
- a universal monk -
embracing & honouring
all faiths & none.

John has been following his own spiritual path all his life, and is guided. He was brought up as a Christian and confirmed at the age of 13. He then went to a Quaker Boarding School for five years and developed his love for the countryside and walking. He became fascinated with Tibet and whilst retaining his Christian roots, became immersed in Buddhism. For four years he studied at the Tara Buddhist Centre in Derbyshire. He progressed into Daoism and currently attends the Chinese Buddhist Temple (Pure Land Tradition) in London. With his thirst for knowledge and discovery he paid attention to other faiths and appreciated their values. Late in life he decided it was time to reveal his spiritual beliefs and practices and discovered the Interfaith Seminary.

'When the pupil is ready, the teacher will appear'. (Buddhist saying).

Here for two years he learnt in more depth the whole spectrum of faiths , including   Jainism, Paganism, Mother Earth, Buddhism, Hinduism, Islam, Judaism, Sikhism, Celtic Worship and Shamanism. This is an ongoing exploration without end. He embraces all faiths, for all have a beauty of their own. All paths/faiths lead to one goal/truth. On July 17th. 2010 he was Ordained as a Multi-faith Minister.

'May you go in peace, with joy in your heart
and may the divine be always at your side.'

Using his knowledge and experience he combines many faiths into a simple, caring and devoted services, individually made for each specific occasion, with dignity and honour.
He conducts special Ceremonies -

Popular Funeral Celebrant and member of the Natural Death Society.

* Funerals * Memorial Services * Sermons * Weddings   *Civil Partnerships
* Baby Blessings & Naming
* Rites of Passage * Healing Ceremonies * Pilgrimages * Inspirational Talks
Qigong Teacher.   Reiki Prationer.

For further information Contact John on -
Tel/Fax: 01992 - 762776   Mobile. 07910 889429
Email - universalmonk@oulook.com
Ministry site -www.thejohnmerrillministry.co.uk
All Faiths church - www.londoninterfaithchurch.co.uk

Revd. John N. Merrill, HonMUni
32, Holmesdale, Waltham Cross,
Hertfordshire EN8 8QY